VERILOG FOR DIGITAL DESIGN

THE WILEY BICENTENNIAL–KNOWLEDGE FOR GENERATIONS

Each generation has its unique needs and aspirations. When Charles Wiley first opened his small printing shop in lower Manhattan in 1807, it was a generation of boundless potential searching for an identity. And we were there, helping to define a new American literary tradition. Over half a century later, in the midst of the Second Industrial Revolution, it was a generation focused on building the future. Once again, we were there, supplying the critical scientific, technical, and engineering knowledge that helped frame the world. Throughout the 20th Century, and into the new millennium, nations began to reach out beyond their own borders and a new international community was born. Wiley was there, expanding its operations around the world to enable a global exchange of ideas, opinions, and know-how.

For 200 years, Wiley has been an integral part of each generation's journey, enabling the flow of information and understanding necessary to meet their needs and fulfill their aspirations. Today, bold new technologies are changing the way we live and learn. Wiley will be there, providing you the must-have knowledge you need to imagine new worlds, new possibilities, and new opportunities.

Generations come and go, but you can always count on Wiley to provide you the knowledge you need, when and where you need it!

WILLIAM J. PESCE
PRESIDENT AND CHIEF EXECUTIVE OFFICER

PETER BOOTH WILEY
CHAIRMAN OF THE BOARD

VERILOG FOR DIGITAL DESIGN

Frank Vahid
University of California, Riverside

Roman Lysecky
University of Arizona

EXECUTIVE PUBLISHER	Don Fowley
ASSOCIATE PUBLISHER	Dan Sayre
SENIOR ACQUISITIONS EDITOR	Catherine Fields Shultz
PROJECT EDITOR	Gladys Soto
EDITORIAL ASSISTANT	Chelsee Pengal
SENIOR PRODUCTION EDITOR	Ken Santor
COVER DESIGNER	Michael St. Martine
BICENTENNIAL LOGO DESIGN	Richard J. Pacifico

This book was set in Adobe Framemaker® by the author and printed and bound by Malloy Inc. The cover was printed by Malloy Inc.

This book is printed on acid free paper. ∞

ISBN-13 978-0-470-05262-4

Printed in the United States of America

10 9 8 7 6 5 4 3 2 1

To my family, Amy, Eric, Kelsi, and Maya. — FV

To my father, Gregory. — RL

Preface

TO THOSE ABOUT TO STUDY VERILOG

Designing computing systems, which have impacted nearly every aspect of modern life, can be an exciting and rewarding endeavor. The approach to designing the digital circuits underlying those computing systems, a task known as digital design, has seen a major paradigm shift during the past decades. The previous approach of drawing a circuit's interconnection of components has been largely replaced by an approach of describing such circuits in a hardware description language (HDL), and even by an approach of just describing the desired behavior of such circuits in an HDL and letting tools automatically generate the circuits. The net result is that while designer productivity in the early 1980s was about 100-transistors per month, designer productivity in the 2000s exceeds 10,000 transistors per month and is continuing to increase.

In past decades, digital design was used to create microprocessors, and to create the small "glue logic" circuits that allowed microprocessors and other components to interact with surrounding components. While those uses are still common today, digital design has grown to also include creation of high-performance custom circuit implementations of complex digital processing systems, such as modems, network routers and switches, wireless encrypters, and more. Even computations traditionally executed on microprocessors are increasingly migrating to "coprocessor" or "accelerator" digital circuits that enable high-performance applications previously not possible, such as circuits that perform real-time three-dimensional graphics rendering, decode compressed video streams for cell phone video displays, perform real-time speech understanding or face recognition, or analyze huge amounts of biological data in hours rather than months. Such circuits can also result in low power, small size, and/or decreased costs, depending on the application.

In short, digital design is an exciting and important field of study, and HDLs form the the basis of modern digital design. Learning an HDL can thus prove a worthwhile endeavor. Verilog is one of the most widely-used HDLs. Once having learned Verilog, learning a different HDL requires only a fraction of the time, as many basic concepts are similar across different HDLs, especially when using an HDL in a highly-structured manner as introduced in this book.

TO TEACHERS OF VERILOG

Teachers may note that this book differs somewhat from traditional HDL books—the book emphasizes *design* rather than language. Traditional books are organized by language constructs, perhaps introducing data types, then modules, then operators, etc. This book is instead organized by design concepts, starting with combinational design, then basic sequential design, then datapath component design, and finally, register-transfer level design (even touching on algorithmic-level design). The book introduces language constructs as they are needed, being careful to ensure that the most important constructs are covered at some point. The design-based approach may prove more intuitive to students and hence useful to the learning process. The book does contain a mini-reference in the last chapter so that the book can also serve as a reasonable reference for the most important constructs of the language.

The book also clearly distinguishes design (i.e., synthesis) concepts from simulation concepts. This distinction is critical to proper use of an HDL for design, and ultimately it is the design purpose of an HDL that is typically of primary interest when learning an HDL. The book uses a highly-structured approach for describing synthesizable code, which can reduce mismatches between simulation and synthesis, and improve designer efficiency.

This book was created with two key uses in mind. One use is in a digital design course, as a supplement to a digital design textbook. For that use, the book provides a more thorough introduction to HDL concepts than is possible when HDL concepts are instead contained inside a digital design textbook. The authors do not believe that any existing digital design textbook with integrated HDL coverage provides a sufficient introduction to HDLs. A sufficient HDL introduction—which covers different design abstraction levels, including structural and behavioral design, synthesis concepts, simulation concepts, testbench concepts, and more—requires about 150–200 pages, which would overly-enlarge most digital design textbooks. (Furthermore, the authors believe that the student is best served by a digital design book that has the student learn key concepts using the most intuitive means, such as using circuits, truth tables, and state diagrams, before introducing the additional layer of indirection present in HDLs). Likewise, the authors have found that standalone HDL books having 300–600 pages are too lengthy, detailed, and costly for effective use as a supplement in a digital design course. A few short (200–250 page) introductory HDL books do exist, but we have found them to be language-oriented rather than design oriented. Language-orientation leads to the common situation of students writing HDL code that simulates fine, and then expressing frustration and bewilderment when that code does not synthesize correctly. While this book can be used as a supplement to any digital design textbook, it ideally supplements the textbook *Digital Design* by Frank Vahid (John Wiley and Sons, Inc.), following the same chapter structure, using the same terminology, and using many of the same examples.

The second use of this book is as a standalone HDL introduction. The authors believe that the concepts covered are ideally suited as an introduction, enough to enable straightforward structured design of combinational logic, sequential logic, datapath components, and register-transfer level designs, but not so much as to overwhelm the reader with advanced constructs. As such, this book may serve well in a first course on HDL-based design, which is typically an upper-division undergraduate or even graduate level course. A second course on HDL-based design might use a lengthier HDL book.

ABOUT THE BOOK

CHAPTER OVERVIEW

This book is about digital design using an HDL. Its chapters cover increasingly complex digital design concepts and introduces HDL constructs as they are needed. After Chapter 1 introduces HDL-based design, Chapter 2 discusses basic combinational logic design, and Chapter 3 discusses basic sequential logic design. Chapter 4 introduces the design of some common datapath components, such that other datapath components could easily be described using similar techniques. Chapter 5 introduces register-transfer level (RTL) design, the design level at which the majority of digital designs are described in HDLs today. Finally, Chapter 6 provides a mini-reference to the most common HDL constructs. Most of those constructs were introduced in the earlier chapters, but Chapter 6 provides a handy means for quickly looking up the key aspects of each language construct, as well as serving as a good review after reading the earlier chapters. Chapter 6 also provides coverage of a few advanced constructs that are often useful for larger HDL designs.

Because the same HDL is typically used for both design (synthesis) purposes and for purely simulation purposes (as in a testbench for testing a design), subsections that deal specifically with synthesis or with simulation are noted as such using special icons next to the subsection headings, namely with ↓ for synthesis and with ⎍⎍ for simulation.

ACCOMPANYING RESOURCES

This book contains several accompanying resources and related items.

All HDL code in the text comes from complete Verilog files that have been compiled and simulated with a commercial Verilog simulator, and that code is available to users of this book.

The book comes with a complete set of graphical, carefully-colored, animated PowerPoint slides. Every figure in the book comes from a figure in the slides. The slides may prove very useful to the reader as a learning tool—readers may in fact find that a good approach to learning the HDL is to first progress through the animated slides, and then refer to the book for a more in-depth explanation. Teachers may find that the slides serve as a truly useful teaching tool in their lectures and lab/discussion sections. It might interest teachers to know that the authors actually developed the slides *first*, before writing the book itself—the authors consider the slides to be a critical part of the complete teaching package, rather than an afterthought.

A 550-page introductory digital design textbook whose chapters and examples largely match those in this book is available for in-depth study of the digital design concepts in this book.

A matching book that has the same structure and examples but that introduces the VHDL language, titled "VHDL for Digital Design", is also available.

HDLs are best learned through experience, and thus readers are strongly encouraged to actively use an HDL simulator while learning the material in this book. Fortunately, free or low-cost versions of several high-quality commercial simulators have become available in recent years.

Information on the above resources and items can be found at the book's website, reachable from the site: *http://www.ddvahid.com*.

FORMATTING

The code that appears in the text has been cut-and-pasted directly from tested HDL files. Thus, one may note that the formatting of the HDL code is not as "pretty" as in many other HDL books, which may bold or color HDL keywords in their code samples. However, the authors felt that correctness of the code outweighed any benefits gained from bolded or colored code, which would have required manual retyping or modification of the tested code, and which often explains the subtle mistakes commonly found in the code of many HDL books. Therefore, the book uses the convention of typing all user-defined names as initially capitalized, such as "Input" or "Y", to distinguish them from Verilog keywords, which Verilog requires to be lowercase, such as "input". That convention allowed for the cut-and-paste method of including code in the book, while still distinguishing HDL keywords from user-defined names in the code. The authors point out, however, that HDL coders need not use the initially-capitalized user-defined name convention, as most HDL-entry tools automatically bold or color the keywords for a designer.

The text in this book intentionally violates the basic English punctuation rule of placing sentence punctuation within quoted text, such as the final period in the quoted text: "Hello." In this book, such text would appear as: "Hello". For normal English, the punctuation rule is a bit inelegant (at least to some of us computer-language folks), but when quoting HDL code, the rule could cause great confusion. HDL code samples in this book will thus be shown as follows: "*x = 0;*". The alternative, with sentence punctuation within the quotes, could have confused the reader into thinking that the sentence punctuation is part of the HDL code, as in: "*x = 0;*." In that code example, a reader may think that the period is part of the HDL code.

ACKNOWLEDGMENTS

We would like to thank John Wiley and Sons publishers, and in particular Gladys Soto and Catherine Shultz, for their support of this book. We thank Scott Sirowy and David Sheldon for their proofreading assistance. We thank Brian Alleyne of Cisco Systems for his helpful input, and we thank the many engineers from Intel, IBM, Motorola, Freescale, and Xilinx, with whom we have worked during the years and who have in one way or another contributed to the concepts in this book. The research support from the National Science Foundation has also been instrumental in providing a solid foundation for the authors and is thus acknowledged with sincere gratitude.

ABOUT THE AUTHORS

Frank Vahid is a Professor of Computer Science and Engineering at the University of California, Riverside, and is the Associate Director of the Center for Embedded Computer Systems at the University of California, Irvine. He received his B.S. in Computer Engineering from the University of Illinois in 1988, and his M.S. and Ph.D. in Computer Science from the University of California, Irvine in 1990 and 1994, respectively. He has taught, researched, worked, and consulted in the field of digital design since 1986. His experience with HDLs includes not only writing an HDL compiler and developing numerous HDL-based synthesis tools, but also includes writing many thousands of lines of HDL code for synthesis. He has authored the textbooks "Specification and Design of Embedded Systems (Prentice-Hall, 1994), "Embedded System Design: A Unified Hardware/Software Introduction" (John Wiley and Sons, 2001), and "Digital Design" (John Wiley and Sons, 2007). He has published over 150 research papers, chaired the ISSS and the CODES symposia in the field of embedded system design, held engineering positions at Hewlett Packard and AMCC, consulted for numerous companies including Motorola and NEC, holds several U.S. patents, and conducts collaborative digital design research with several companies including Intel, IBM, Freescale, and Xilinx.

Roman Lysecky is an Assistant Professor of Electrical and Computer Engineering at the University of Arizona. He received his B.S., M.S., and Ph.D. in Computer Science from the University of California, Riverside in 1999, 2000, and 2005, respectively. His expertise in HDLs and synthesis of digital designs includes writing tens of thousands of lines of synthesizable HDL code, including several microprocessor designs, a high-performance profiler, dozens of hardware coprocessors for multimedia, automotive, and digital signal processing applications, a multi-channel DMA controller, as well as a custom FPGA architecture, all synthesized as ASIC or FPGA circuits. He has extensive experience with simulation and synthesis tools from Synopsys, Cadence, Mentor Graphics, Aldec, and Xilinx, including synthesizing a custom FPGA architecture, described using an HDL, as a 0.13μm circuit, simulated and verified at the post-layout level in collaboration with Intel. He has developed several computer-aided design tools for ASICs and FPGAs, including logic synthesis, technology mapping, and place and route tools. He has published many research papers, receiving the Best Paper Award at the Design Automation and Test in Europe Conference (DATE) and the outstanding Ph.D. dissertation award from the European Design and Automation Association in 2006, and he holds one U.S. patent.

Contents

CHAPTER 1

Introduction

1.1 DIGITAL SYSTEMS

Digital systems surround us, being present in almost any modern device that uses electricity. A ***digital system*** is an electronic system that operates on two-valued electric signals, referred to as *'1'* and *'0'*. The most common implementation of digital systems today is on an ***integrated circuit***, or IC, also known as a "chip." Figure 1.1 shows an IC package whose cover had been removed, revealing the normally-hidden IC inside, surrounded by the package's pins that connect to the IC's perimeter.

Figure 1.1 An integrated circuit (IC).

The most widely-known digital systems are computers, such as desktop computers ("PCs") and laptop computers, shown in Figure 1.2(a). However, digital systems appear inside a multitude of other devices, such as those in Figure 1.2(b), including:

- Consumer electronics: Cell phones, portable music players, cameras, video game consoles, electronic music instruments, etc.
- Medical equipment: Hearing aids, pacemakers, life support systems, etc.

(a) (b)

Figure 1.2 Digital system examples: (a) computers, (b) diverse electronic devices.

- Automotive electronics: Engine control, anti-lock brakes, navigation systems, cruise controllers, etc.
- And much more: Military equipment, networking equipment, office electronics, etc.

Such digital systems, which are embedded within larger electronic devices, are often referred to as ***embedded systems***.

1.2 HARDWARE DESCRIPTION LANGUAGES

Digital systems have become increasingly complex during the past several decades. This increase in complexity is due to what is known as Moore's Law—the trend of ICs doubling their capacity to hold digital components (i.e., transistors) roughly every 18 months, illustrated in Figure 1.3. In the 1960s and 1970s, typical ICs might have contained tens to thousands of transistors. In the 1980s, capacities increased to the hundreds of thousands. The 1990s saw capacities in the tens of millions. ICs of the 2000s reached into the billions of transistors per IC.

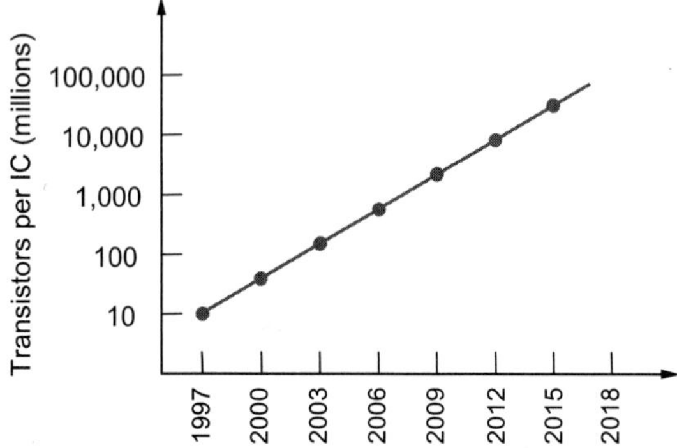

Figure 1.3 IC capacities have doubled roughly every 18 months (Moore's Law), leading to increasingly complex ICs.

In the 1970s, after an IC was built, the IC's behavior would be documented through a combination of schematics (circuit drawings), diagrams, and natural language (such as English) descriptions, as illustrated in Figure 1.4. The size of such documentation commonly reached hundreds of pages. Engineers that purchased ICs to use in their own systems would have to read that documentation to understand the behavior of the ICs, so that those engineers could properly design other systems that interfaced with the ICs. However, reading hundreds of pages of documentation was hard. Furthermore, that documentation often contained errors and ambiguities. Engineers using ICs thus often had trouble integrating those ICs with other ICs, and with other devices in their systems.

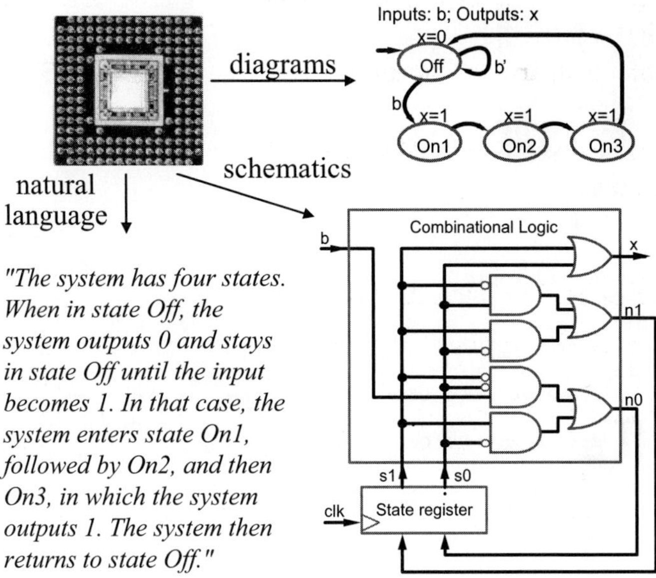

Figure 1.4 ICs of the 1970s were documented using schematics, diagrams, and natural language descriptions, resulting in hundreds of pages of documentation.

Another problem facing designers was that of ensuring a design was correct before actually implementing the design as an IC. Simulating the design before implementation could help. ***Simulation*** is a procedure wherein a tool, known as a simulator, automatically generates output values of a hardware module for a given sequence of input values. Most simulators at that time took schematics as their design input. However, schematics can be difficult to work with when dealing with large circuits. Some people at the time believed that textual languages would be more efficient, and thus began developing hardware description languages. A ***hardware description language***, or ***HDL***, is a machine-readable and human-readable textual language for describing hardware. An HDL is precise and can thus be automatically simulated to see exactly how an IC is supposed to behave. Figure 1.5 illustrates how an HDL could be used to describe the behavior of an IC, and then simulated to create output values for given input values.

In the early to mid 1980s, several groups were working on developing HDLs. The Verilog HDL and a Verilog simulator were developed at a company called Gateway Design Automation in the mid-1980s. Verilog was developed to have a syntax similar to the C programming language, which was the most popular software programming language in industry in the 1980s. Gateway Design Automation was later acquired by Cadence Design Systems, who thereby acquired the Verilog language and simulator. In the early 1990s, Cadence made Verilog an open rather than proprietary language, and Verilog eventually became IEEE standard number 1364 in the year 1995. IEEE stands for the Institute of Electrical and Electronics Engineers.

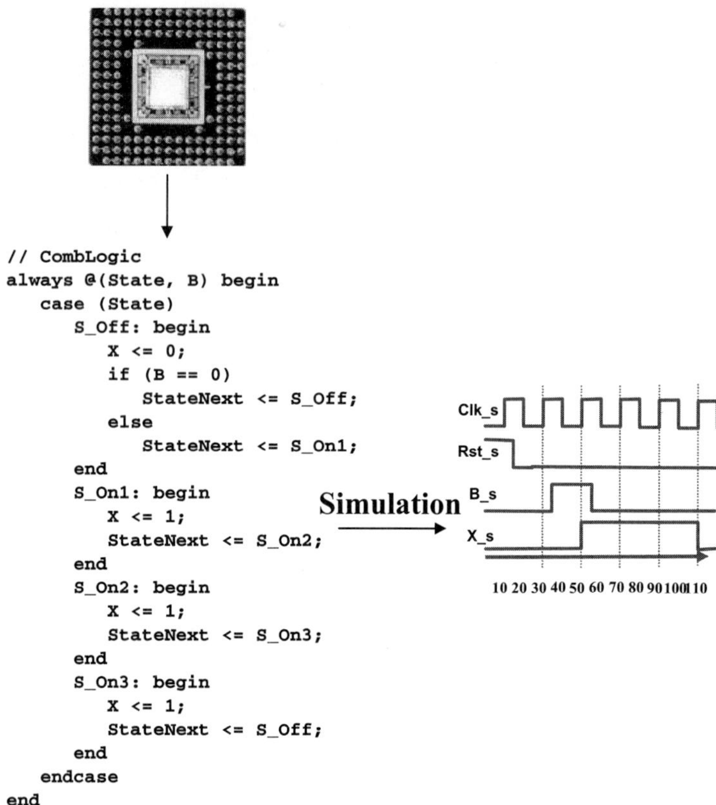

Figure 1.5 An HDL provides a precise machine-readable description of the behavior of an IC, enabling simulation and hence clear knowledge of how an IC's outputs would react to a given sequence of inputs.

Verilog is one of several popular modern HDLs. Another HDL, VHDL, was also developed in the mid-1980s, through a project of the U.S. Department of Defense. ***VHDL*** stands for the *VHSIC **H**ardware **D**escription **L**anguage*. *VHSIC* itself stands for *Very High Speed Integrated Circuit*, which was a project of the DoD. VHDL has a syntax similar to the Ada language, a software programming language whose development was also spurred by the DoD in the late 1970s. VHDL became IEEE standard number 1076 in 1987.

A third HDL, SystemC, has recently evolved. The continued capacity increases of ICs resulted in the increasingly common situation of multiple microprocessors and custom hardware circuits co-existing on a single IC. Such system-on-a-chip ICs require integrated simulation of both microprocessor software and custom circuit hardware. Some tools, known as *co-simulators*, evolved in the 1990s seeking to link hardware simulations (using languages like VHDL or Verilog) with microprocessor simulators (executing code written in languages like C or C++). As another option to using such tools, SystemC was developed in the 2000s by several companies seeking to develop a single language suitable for efficiently simulating all of a system's software and hardware components using a single language and simulation

```
module DoorOpener(C,H,P,F);
   input C, H, P;
   output F;
   reg F;

   always @(C,H,P)
   begin
      F <= (~C) & (H | P);
   end
endmodule
```

(a)

```
ENTITY DoorOpener IS
   PORT (c, h, p: IN std_logic;
         f: OUT std_logic);
END DoorOpener;

ARCHITECTURE Beh OF DoorOpener IS
BEGIN
   PROCESS(c, h, p)
   BEGIN
      f <= NOT(c) AND (h OR p);
   END PROCESS;
END Beh;
```

(b)

```
#include "systemc.h"
SC_MODULE(DoorOpener)
{
   sc_in<sc_logic> c, h, p;
   sc_out<sc_logic> f;

   SC_CTOR(DoorOpener)
   {
      SC_METHOD(comblogic);
      sensitive << c << h << p;
   }

   void comblogic()
   {
      f.write((~c.read()) & (h.read() | p.read()));
   }
};
```

(c)

Figure 1.6 HDL descriptions of a simple circuit: (a) Verilog, (b) VHDL, and (c) SystemC.

environment. SystemC consists of libraries and macro routines added to the popular C++ object-oriented software programming language. Some people argue that SystemC is not really a hardware description language, but rather a system description language. SystemC became IEEE standard number 1666 in the year 2005. SystemC is a bit cumbersome for describing low-level hardware, but excels at system-level descriptions.

Figure 1.6 illustrates the description of a simple circuit's behavior in Verilog, VHDL, and SystemC.

SystemVerilog is another system-modeling language. It is an extension of Verilog with the intent of dealing with whole-chip modeling issues. Various extensions deal with supporting calls to or from C/C++/SystemC functions, making bus descriptions easier and more efficient, supporting assertion-based descriptions that check for correct design behavior, and providing some object-oriented features especially well-suited for making testbenches. SystemVerilog became IEEE standard number 1800 in the year 2005.

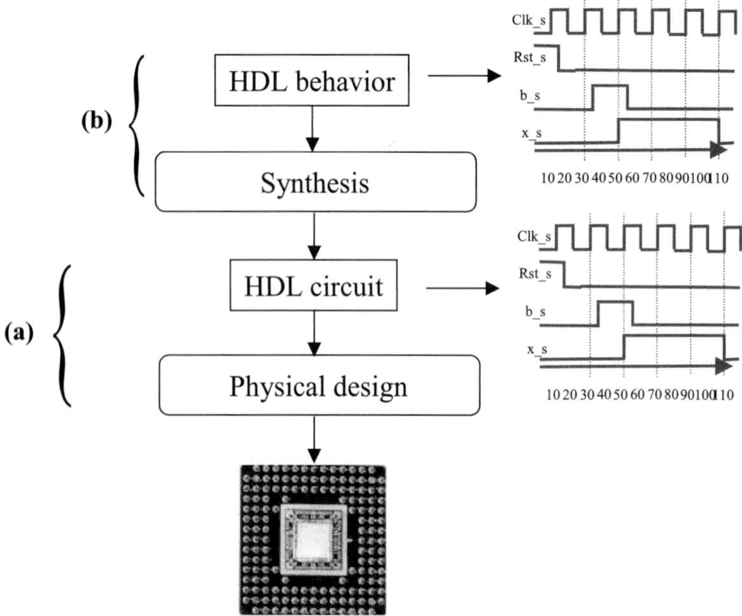

Figure 1.7 Evolution of HDLs as a design and synthesis language, rather than just a documentation language: (a) used to describe a circuit, followed by evolution of physical design tools to convert circuits to IC implementations, (b) used to describe desired behavior, followed by evolution of synthesis tools that automatically convert such behavior to circuits.

1.3 HDLS FOR DESIGN AND SYNTHESIS

Although Verilog was originally used primarily as a language for simulating an existing circuit, the language evolved to be used for design and synthesis. ***Design*** refers to converting a higher-level description of a system to a lower-level description representing an implementation. Designers used HDLs to describe circuits as inputs to simulation, to ensure correct behavior, as in Figure 1.7(a). With HDL circuit descriptions common, *physical design* tools evolved to convert HDL descriptions to IC implementations, reducing designer effort.

Furthermore, designers increasingly began to use HDLs to describe the intended circuit behavior before designing those circuits, as in Figure 1.7(b). Designers simulated those behavioral descriptions first to ensure correct functionality. Those behavioral descriptions were far simpler than circuit descriptions, allowing the designer to focus on high-level functional concepts ("What should happen if these two inputs become *'1'* at the same time?") before dealing with low-level issues ("Should this register be connected to that logic gate?"). Designers then converted the behavioral description into a circuit description, and simulated again, with the expectation that the two simulations would match. ***Synthesis tools*** evolved to automatically convert behavioral descriptions into circuit descriptions.

This book focuses on the use of Verilog for design (rather than documentation), with a heavy emphasis on the language's use for synthesis. Many people learning Verilog are doing so to be able use synthesis tools, such as tools that synthesize Verilog code for implementation as an ASIC (application-specific integrated circuit) or field-programmable gate array (FPGA). A ***field-programmable gate array (FPGA)*** is an increasingly popular type of off-the-shelf IC that can be configured to implement custom circuits merely by programming the IC with a series of bits, akin to programming a microprocessor IC. The increasing popularity of FPGAs has significantly increased the importance of HDLs. However, Verilog is a general language intended for simulation as well as for synthesis. Therefore, not all Verilog code that simulates can also be synthesized by synthesis tools. As a simple example, Verilog supports description of delays, but modern synthesis tools don't use such delay information in creating circuits. New Verilog users may write code that simulates correctly, but that does not synthesize to the expected circuit. Those users often conclude that the synthesis tools are weak or faulty. While some tools may indeed be weak or faulty, in many cases the problem is that the Verilog code was not reasonably written for synthesis purposes.

As an analogy, consider a natural language like English. On the one hand, English is a very general language, suitable for a variety of purposes including conversation, textbooks, jokes, poetry, and cooking recipes. On the other hand, the specific purpose of recipes involves a highly-specialized use of the language. A reasonable recipe might use words like stir, blend, eggs, and bowl, but would not use words like bludgeon, harmonic, forthright, and castigate. A recipe using the latter words may represent correct English grammar, but if the food doesn't turn out well, we should not blame the chef.

Likewise, Verilog is a very general language, suitable for a variety of purposes. But when used for synthesis, the language must be used in a disciplined restricted manner.

Many Verilog textbooks introduce the Verilog language first, construct by construct, and then later describe how to use the language for synthesis. However, if one seeks to learn the English language primarily for the purpose of writing recipes in English, learning the entire English language first is not necessarily the best approach. Likewise, if one seeks to learn the Verilog language for the purpose of synthesis, learning the entire Verilog language first is not necessarily the best approach either. Not only would learning the general language involve extraneous information not central to one's purpose, but even the relevant information being learned might be better understood if introduced in the context of the desired purpose—clear motivating examples often enhance learning.

This book therefore differs from many other introductory Verilog books. Rather than being organized around Verilog language constructs, the book is instead organized around increasingly complex digital design tasks: Combinational logic design, sequential logic design, datapath component design, and finally register-transfer level (RTL) design. For each design task, the book introduces the Verilog constructs necessary to accomplish those tasks. In summary, the book is designed as an introduction to using Verilog for digital design, rather than as a reference book on the Verilog language. Nevertheless, through use of the mini-reference chapter and the extensive index at the end of the book, this book can also serve as a useful reference book.

This *Verilog for Digital Design* book can be used as a standalone introduction to Verilog. However, this book was also created to be easily used as a supplement to the textbook *Digital Design* by Frank Vahid, published by John Wiley and Sons, Inc. The chapters of this book follow the *Digital Design* textbook's chapter organization, and many of the examples come from that textbook too. A learning of digital design via the *Digital Design* textbook can be supplemented by following the study of each textbook chapter with a study of this book's corresponding chapter, e.g., following *Digital Design* Chapter 2 by this book's Chapter 2, following *Digital Design* Chapter 3 by this book's Chapter 3, and so on for Chapters 4 and 5 too.

The book is organized as follows. Chapter 2 introduces the description in Verilog of basic combinational components. Chapter 3 introduces the description of basic sequential components. Chapter 4 covers description techniques for datapath components, both combinational and sequential. Chapter 5 describes register-transfer level design. Throughout each chapter, Verilog constructs are introduced as they are needed, as are key HDL concepts such as building a testbench, understanding how a simulator works, and debugging. Furthermore, each chapter stresses a top-down design approach, wherein components are first described behaviorally, and then refined into a structural description. Chapter 6 is a mini-reference that summarizes the Verilog constructs introduced in the book in one convenient place.

CHAPTER 2

Combinational Logic Design

2.1 *AND*, *OR*, AND *NOT* GATES

AND, OR, and NOT gates are the basic components of digital design. We begin by showing how to define and simulate those gate components.[1]

MODULES AND PORTS

Defining a new component in Verilog begins by defining a new module. A ***module*** is the main hardware abstraction in Verilog, having inputs, outputs, and a well-defined function.

A module definition begins as shown in Figure 2.1 for a 2-input AND, a 2-input OR, and a NOT component (also known as an inverter). The beginning defines the module's *interface* to the outside world, including the module's name and the module's inputs and outputs. The description in Figure 2.1 names the modules *And2*, *Or2*, and *Inv*, respectively. Those names could have been different ones, like *Fred*, *George*, and *Bob*, but the names *And2*, *Or2*, and *Inv* are more descriptive of the items being created.

A module's inputs and outputs, known as ***ports,*** appear in a list contained between the parentheses just after the module's name, as in "*module And2(X, Y, F);*". Each port must then appear in an ***input*** or ***output*** declaration to indicate the port's direction, as in "*input X, Y;*". In Figure 2.1, all the ports are of type ***bit***, which at this point can be considered to hold either a value of *0* or *1*, or an unknown value of *x*.

[1]Verilog actually has primitives for those gates built into the language, but it is instructive to define them ourselves to help learn the language and to learn simulation concepts.

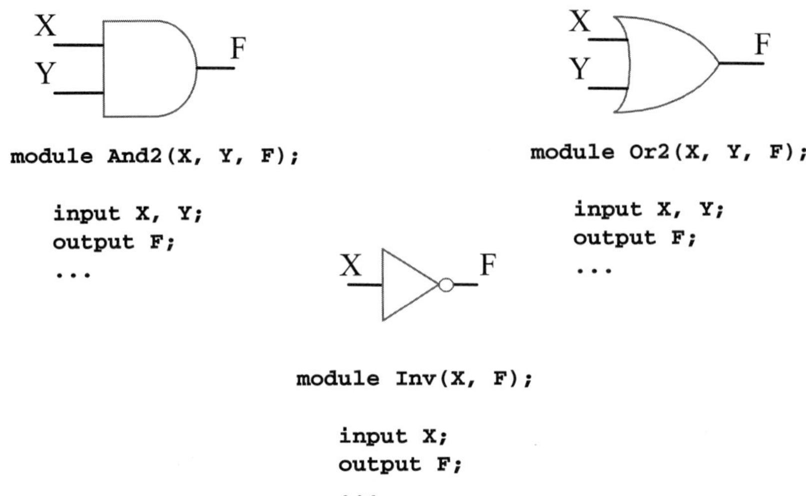
X
Y
F
module And2(X, Y, F);
input X, Y;
output F;
...
X
Y
F
module Or2(X, Y, F);
input X, Y;
output F;
...
X
F
module Inv(X, F);
input X;
output F;
...

Figure 2.1 Beginning of module definitions for AND, OR, and NOT (Inv) gates.

The Verilog code in Figure 2.1 consists of several keywords and several user-defined names. A ***keyword*** (sometimes called a *reserved word*) is an identifier that has special significance in the language and may not be used as a user-defined name. Verilog keywords appearing in Figure 2.1 are *module*, *input*, and *output*. Keywords must be **lower case**, not UPPER CASE or a MixTure thereof. ***User-defined names*** are identifiers used to describe parts of a design. User-defined names appearing in Figure 2.1 are *And2*, *Or2*, *Inv*, *X*, *Y*, and *F*. User-defined names must start with a letter or underscore (_), optionally followed by any sequence of letters, digits, underscores, or dollar signs ($). Examples of valid and invalid user-defined names include:

- Valid names: *A, X, Hello, JXYZ, B14, Sig432, Wire_23, _F1, F$2, _Go_$_$, _, Input.* Note: Some of these names, like "_" and "*Input*", are valid, but unwise.
- Invalid names: *input* (keyword), *$ab* (doesn't start with letter or underscore), *2A* (doesn't start with letter or underscore)

Verilog is ***case sensitive***, meaning there is a difference between upper and lower-case letters. For example, the identifier *Sig432* is different from *SIG432* and from *sig432*. In this book, we will follow the convention of starting all user-defined names with a capital letter, such as *Sig432*, to distinguish user-defined names from keywords (which are lower case). Most Verilog editors will automatically bold or color keywords, diminishing the benefit of initially capitalizing identifiers. However, for the Verilog shown in this book, we use initially capitalized user-defined names to enhance clarity.

Example 2.1: Module definition beginning for a 4x1 multiplexor

A 4x1 mux has four data inputs, two select inputs, and a data output. We can name them *I3*, *I2*, *I1*, *I0*, *S1*, *S0*, and *D*, and we can name the module *Mux4*, as shown in Figure 2.2(a). Figure 2.2(b) shows the beginning of a module definition using those names. Ports *I3*, *I2*, *I1*, and *I0* are grouped into one input declaration, and ports *S1* and *S0* into another, to enhance readability.

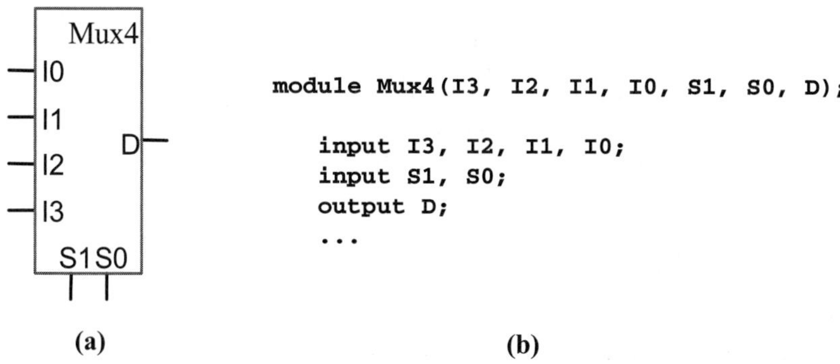
Mux4
I0
I1
I2
I3
D
S1 S0
(a)
module Mux4(I3, I2, I1, I0, S1, S0, D);
input I3, I2, I1, I0;
input S1, S0;
output D;
...
(b)

Figure 2.2 4x1 mux: (a) block diagram, (b) module definition beginning.

MODULE PROCEDURES—ALWAYS

While the beginning of a module defines the module's *interface* to the outside world, the remainder defines what is *inside* the module. In other words, the remainder describes the module's function, namely, how the module's outputs are related to the inputs. Notice in Figure 2.1 that the inputs and outputs of the *And2* module and of the *Or2* module are identical to one another; the remainder of the module definition describes how those modules differ.

Figure 2.3 shows a complete module definition for an *And2* module. Many ways exist to describe the contents of a module. One way uses an "always" procedure. A ***procedure*** is a sequence of statements executed by a simulator one statement at a time, starting from the first statement. An ***always procedure*** is a procedure that is executed at the start of simulation, and then repeated. *An always procedure thus describes an infinite loop.*

The *always* procedure in Figure 2.3 begins with "*always @(X,Y) begin*", meaning the procedure only executes its statements if the value of *X* changes or the value of *Y* changes, where "*@(X,Y)*" defines the procedure's event control. The ***event control*** of a procedure indicates that the procedure should only execute its statements when at least one of the listed events occurs. A change of value of a listed item is considered an ***event***. The list is

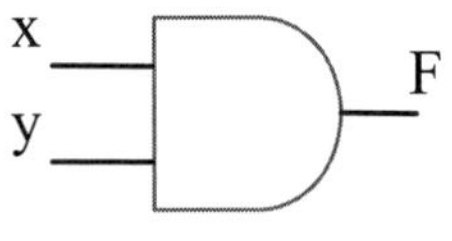


```
module And2(X, Y, F);

   input X, Y;
   output F;
   reg F;

   always @(X, Y) begin
      F <= X & Y;
   end

endmodule
```

wait until X or Y changes

F <= x AND y

Figure 2.3 Module definition for a 2-input AND gate named *And2*.

often called a *sensitivity list*, and the procedure is said to be ***sensitive*** to the listed items. The events are separated by commas, although Verilog also allows separation using the keyword ***or***. Thus, whenever *X* or *Y* changes, the procedure executes its statements, and then waits for another change on either *X* or *Y* before executing its statements again.

The procedure contains a single statement, "*F <= X & Y;*", which computes the bitwise AND of *X* and *Y*, and assigns the result (either *0* or *1*) to *F*. *&* is a built-in bitwise AND operator. "<=" is the symbol for assigning a value to a port (or any variable; more later). That symbol consists of two characters, "<" and "=", intended to create the appearance of an arrow pointing to the left. Procedures will be described in more detail later.

Before the procedure, the declaration "*reg F;*" appears. That declaration declares output port *F* to be a ***reg*** variable data type. A ***variable*** data type holds its values between assignments. There are several kinds of variables, but presently we only consider the *reg* kind, which stores a bit. The reg declaration is needed to make *F* hold its value between successive executions of the always procedure.[2] More on this subject later.

Figure 2.4 shows module definitions for *Or2* and *Inv* modules. The always procedures use the operators | and ~, both built-in operators representing bitwise OR and NOT, respectively.

[2]"reg" comes from the word register. The naming is unfortunate. A reg variable may or may not correspond to an actual register. There is obviously no register in an AND gate, the subject of the current example.

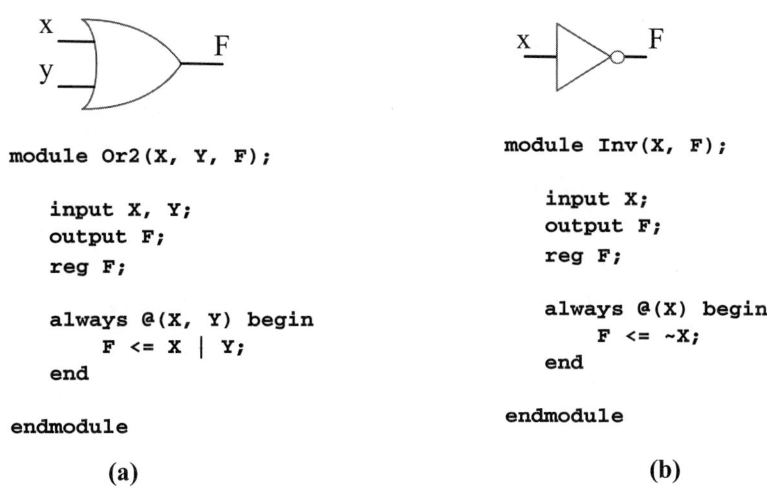

Figure 2.4 Module definitions for: (a) a 2-input OR gate, (b) a 2-input NOT gate (inverter).

[SIMUL] SIMULATION AND TESTBENCHES—A FIRST LOOK

Given a newly-defined module, one may wish to see how the module behaves. In other words, for particular input values, what will be the module's output values? ***Simulation*** is a process wherein a tool, known as a simulator, automatically generates output values for a given module and for a given sequence of input values.

Before applying simulation, a designer must define the sequence of input values that he/she wishes to provide to the module during the simulation. The designer will likely want to provide many different values on each input. For example, for a 2-input AND gate, one might provide input values *YX=00*, *YX=01*, *YX=10*, and *YX=11*, as shown in Figure 2.5(b). Each combination of input values at a particular time is known as a ***test vector***. The figure shows those values graphically, using what are known as ***waveforms***. Some simulators allow users to describe test vectors by drawing waveforms using a graphical tool. The simulator then reads those test vectors and the module definition file shown in Figure 2.5(c), and automatically generates output waveforms, as illustrated in Figure 2.5(d). Note that the module definition file begins with a timescale directive, which we will describe shortly.

Simulators differ in how they allow users to create input waveforms. Rather than using a simulator's waveform creation capabilities, one can instead describe test vectors in an HDL itself, as illustrated in Figure 2.6. The first statement sets *YX=00*. The next statement sets *YX=01*, but is preceded by "#10", which tells the simulator to wait for 10 simulated time units before executing that statement. The resulting test vectors are identical to the vectors defined by the graphical waveforms.

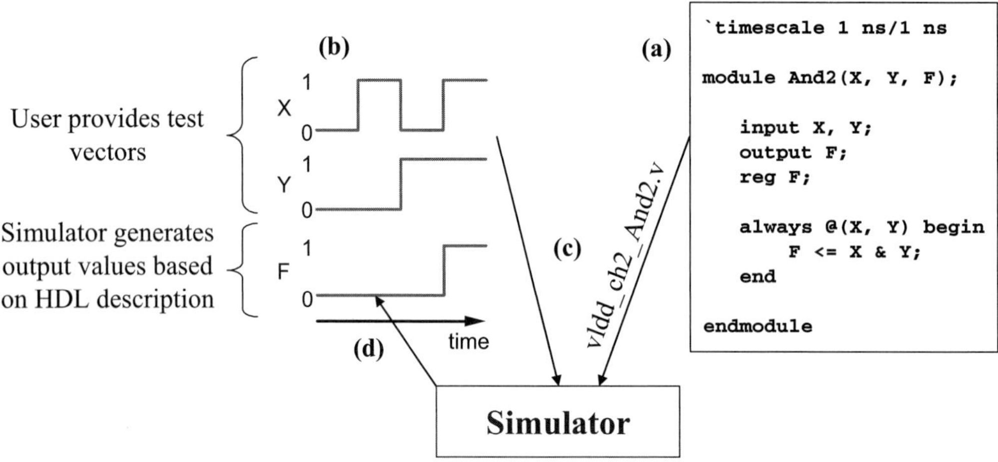

Figure 2.5 Simulating a module: (a) User provides the module definition and (b) the test vectors, (c) simulator reads module definition and test vectors, and (d) simulator generates output values.

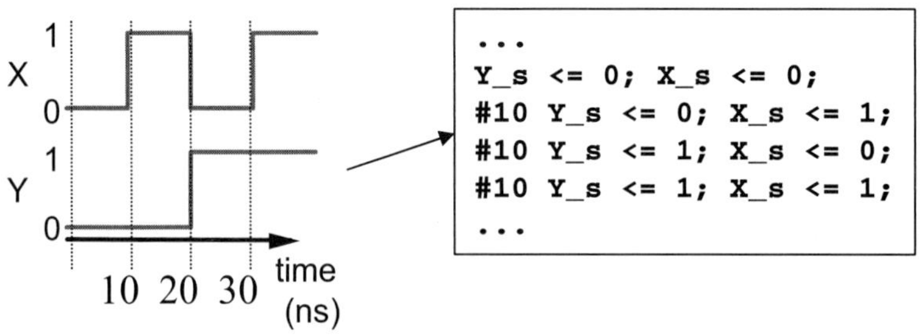

Figure 2.6 Creating test vectors in an HDL.

A ***testbench*** is a setup for applying test vectors to test a design. Figure 2.7 shows the general setup of a testbench. That setup defines a module called *Testbench* having no inputs or outputs. The setup instantiates a module representing the module to be simulated, in this case named *CompToTest* and representing an *And2* module. The setup uses a procedure that writes to variables *X_s* and *Y_s,* which are connected to the inputs of *CompToTest*. The pro-

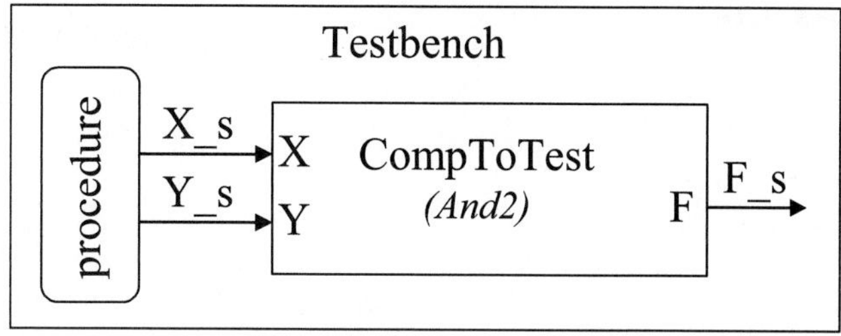

Figure 2.7 General setup of a testbench.

cedure will contain statements that set the variables with the desired test vectors, as was shown in Figure 2.6.

Variables and nets

Figure 2.8 shows a complete Verilog testbench for an *And2* module, following Figure 2.7's setup. The testbench is a module named *Testbench* (although we could have used a different name). The module has no inputs or outputs. The module's contents declare three data items. Two are reg variables *X_s* and *Y_s*, while the third is a wire net *F_s*. Recall that ***reg*** variables store their values between assignments. In contrast, a ***net*** is a data type that does not store a value, but instead that is used for connections, and that derives its value from what it is connected to. There are several types of nets, but we'll only consider ***wire*** nets for now, which represent bits. A testbench should declare reg variables for each input of the module to be tested, and wire nets for each output. The reason is because data items for the inputs will be written by the testbench and thus should hold their value between assignments and thus require reg variables, while data items for the outputs will simply derive their values from the module outputs and thus require wire nets. Variables and nets are needed because a procedure in the testbench module cannot access an instantiated module's ports directly. We'll append "*_s*" to the variables and nets used in a testbench to distinguish them from the ports themselves, although such distinction is not actually required by the language.

The testbench module instantiates one instance of an *And2* module named *CompToTest* and connects the declared variables and nets to the module instance's ports. Section 2.2 will describe variables and nets, instantiation, and port connections in more detail.

Module procedures—initial

The module defines a procedure that sets the *X_s* and *Y_s* variables to particular values at desired times. The procedure type used in Figure 2.8 is an initial procedure. In contrast to the earlier-defined always type of procedure that executes at the simulation start and repeats, an ***initial procedure*** also executes at the simulation start, but only executes once and never repeats.

Testbench format will be discussed further in Section 2.2.

```
`timescale 1 ns/1 ns

module Testbench();

   reg X_s, Y_s;
   wire F_s;

   And2 CompToTest(X_s, Y_s, F_s);

   initial begin
      // Test all possible input combinations
      Y_s <= 0; X_s <= 0;
      #10 Y_s <= 0; X_s <= 1;
      #10 Y_s <= 1; X_s <= 0;
      #10 Y_s <= 1; X_s <= 1;
   end

endmodule
```

Figure 2.8 Testbench for *And2* module.

Delay control

Unlike the procedure of Figure 2.3, the procedure in the testbench of Figure 2.8 has no event control. The first two statements set *Y_s* to *0* and *X_s* to *0*. Note that two statements can appear on one line, but their meaning is the same as if they had appeared on two lines. The following statement has "#10" prepended to it, which is known as a delay control. A ***delay control*** tells the simulator to delay this statement's execution for the specified number of time units. Thus, the procedure of Figure 2.8 effectively holds *Y_s* and *X_s* at "*00*" for ten time units, before executing the next statements, which set *Y_s* and *X_s* to "*01*". The rest of the procedure behaves similarly, holding *Y_s* and *X_s* at "*01*" for ten time units, then at "*10*" for ten time units, before finally setting them to "*11*" and completing execution of the procedure. The procedure's statements thus describe the waveforms for *Y_s* and *X_s* shown in Figure 2.9.

The first line in Figure 2.8's testbench is a ***timescale directive***, which tells the compiler (the program that converts the HDL file to input for a simulator) that from this point forward, 1 time unit corresponds to a particular unit of measurement of time. The particular directive in this case is "*`timescale 1 ns/1 ns*". The grave accent character, "`", indicates that this is a directive to the compiler. Note that the grave accent character is different from an apostrophe or single quote, slanting in the opposite direction. The former "1 ns" indicates that 1 time unit corresponds to 1 ns, or 1 nanosecond. Valid time units are: ***s*** (seconds), ***ms*** (milliseconds), ***us*** (microseconds), ***ns*** (nanoseconds), ***ps*** (picoseconds), and ***fs*** (femtoseconds). The latter 1 ns relates to the precision used during internal time computa-

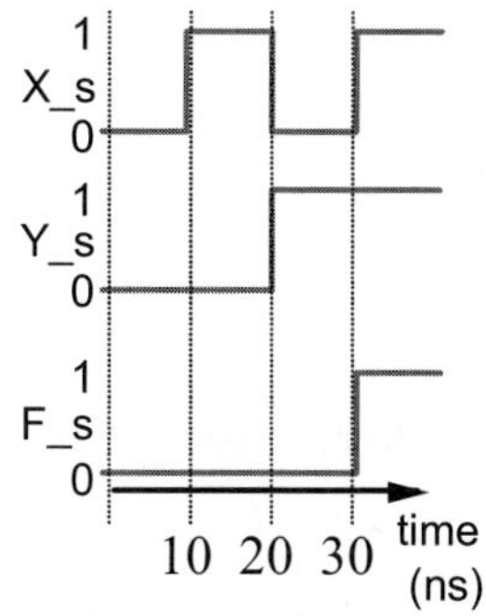

Figure 2.9 Waveforms generated by simulation for an *And2* module.

tions; for our purposes, we'll always make the precision the same as the time unit. Note that all times described above correspond to simulated time, not real time.

One might save the testbench in a file, say *vldd_ch2_And2TB.v*. Providing that file and the *vldd_ch2_And2.v* file to a simulator would then result in the simulator generating the waveforms shown in Figure 2.9. The waveforms show that the module indeed behaves like a 2-input AND gate, outputting *1* only when both inputs are *1*s.

COMMENTS

Figure 2.8 contained the text "*// Test all possible input combinations*". That text is known as a comment. A *comment* is text in HDL code intended only to be read by humans, and not to be read by a simulator or other tool. A comment begins with two forward slashes: "//". All text on the remainder of the same line will be ignored by tools that read the HDL file. Comments enhance the readability of code, primarily by explaining to people the purpose of various parts of the code. In Figure 2.8, the comment makes clear that the test vectors are intended to test all possible combinations of the inputs, something that might otherwise take some time to discern by someone reading the code. Comments should assume the reader understands the language itself, and thus need not state the obvious, such as the comment: "*// Variable and net declarations*". A comment may follow a statement on the same line, such as:

```
L <= 0;   // Turn light on
```

However, the opposite—a statement following a comment on the same line—is not true, because the statement would be considered part of the comment and would thus be ignored.

In addition to explanatory comments throughout code, it is customary to include comments at the top of a file, to describe the file's contents, the author, the authorship date, and other such information.

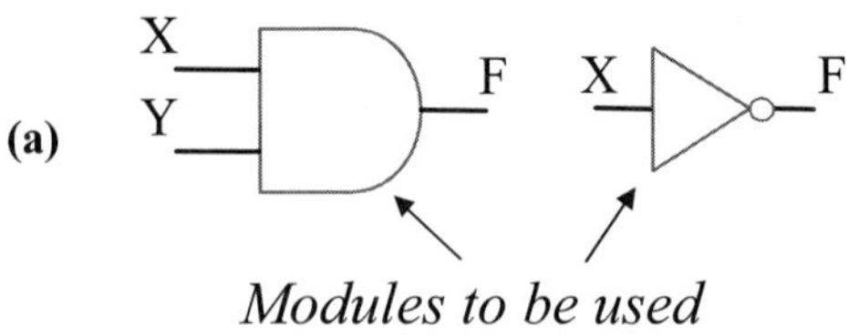

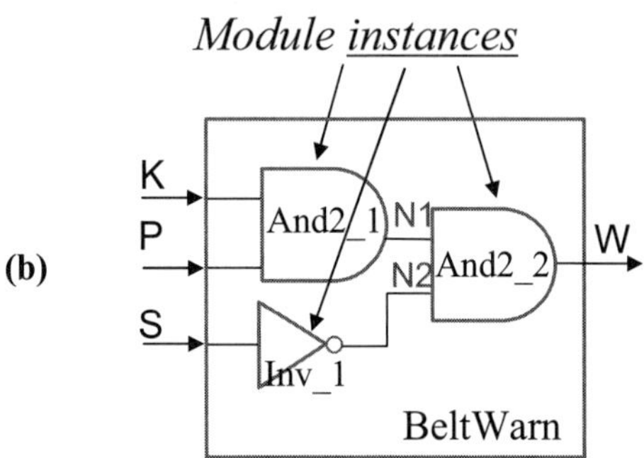

Figure 2.10 Circuit: (a) modules to be used, (b) module instances.

2.2 COMBINATIONAL CIRCUIT STRUCTURE

A ***circuit***, also known as ***structure***, is a connection of modules. Figure 2.10(b) provides an example of a circuit. A circuit represents a second common way of describing the contents of module, in contrast to a procedure as in the previous section.

MODULE INSTANTIATIONS

When used in a circuit, a module—such as an AND, OR, or NOT module defined in the previous section—is known as a ***module instance***. Given the types of modules to be used in a circuit, such as the 2-input AND gate module and the NOT gate (inverter) module shown in Figure 2.10(a), ***instantiating*** a module means to bring into being a unique copy of the module, with each copy known as a module ***instance***. The circuit in Figure 2.10(b) has two instances of a two-input AND gate module, and one instance of a NOT gate module. As an everyday example of instances, a car is built from several types of modules, such as tires, engines, and windows. A car may have four tire instances, one engine instance, and six window instances.

Consider creating a new module that turns on a warning light (by setting an output *W* to *1*) if a car's key is in the car's ignition slot (indicated by an input *K* being *1*), and a passenger is seated (indicated by an input *P* being *1*), and the passenger's seat belt is not buckled (indicated by an input *S* being *0*). One way to define such an module is to use the circuit shown in Figure 2.10(b).

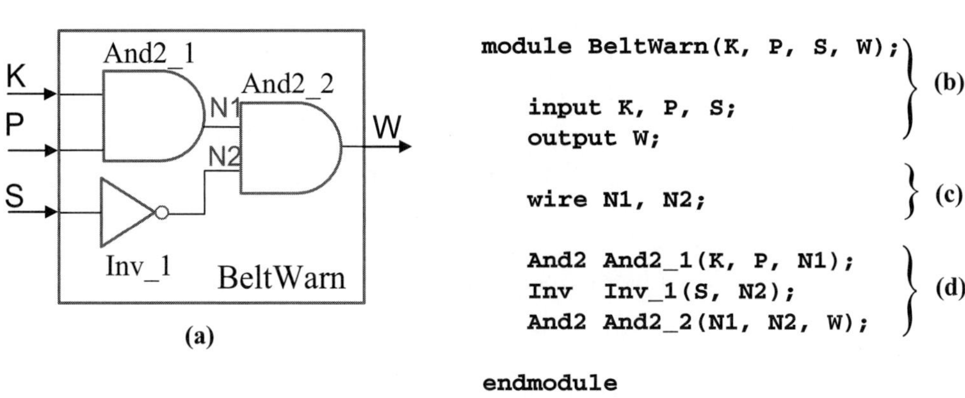

Figure 2.11 Module contents defined as a circuit for the *BeltWarn* module: (a) desired circuit, (b) module definition start, (c) wire declarations, and (d) module instantiations.

Creating a new module defined as a circuit, like the circuit in Figure 2.10(b), involves several steps:

1. Declare a new module with the desired inputs and outputs, as in Figure 2.11(b).
2. Declare internal wires to be used to connect the modules, as in Figure 2.11(c). To do this step, we might first draw the desired circuit so that we know how many internal wires we'll need, and we should create unique names for each internal wire, as in Figure 2.11(a).
3. Instantiate modules and create connections, as in Figure 2.11(d). To do this, we should have created unique names for each module instance in our drawn circuit, as in Figure 2.11(a).

The last step uses module instantiation statements. A ***module instantiation*** statement, shown in Figure 2.12, creates a single instance of a module in a circuit, and describes how that instance connects with circuit wires.

The first part of the module instantiation statement indicates the type of module being instantiated, and the second part gives a unique name for the module instance. Figure 2.11(d) instantiates three module instances: an instance named *And2_1* of type *And2*, an instance named *Inv_1* of type *Inv*, and an instance named *And2_2* of type *And2*. Using numbers at the end of the instance names (e.g., "*_1*" or "*_2*") is one way to create unique

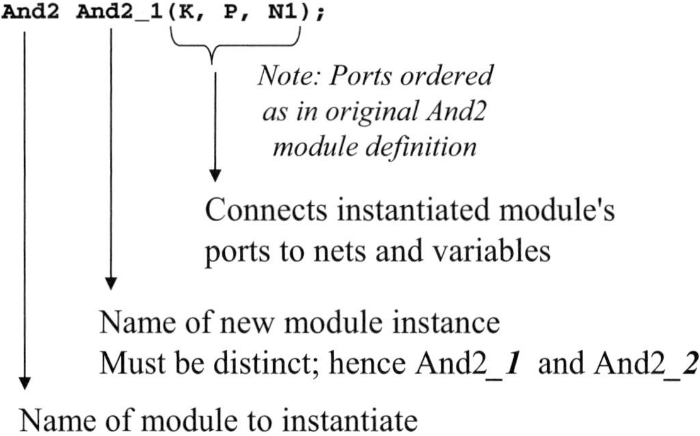

Figure 2.12 Module instantiation statement.

names. Note that any unique identifiers could have been used for the instance names, such as *Comp1*, *Comp2*, and *Comp3*.

PORT CONNECTIONS

The third part of a module instantiation statement, further illustrated in Figure 2.12, is the port connections part. The ***port connections*** part of a module instantiation statement connects the module instance's ports to the variables and nets in the circuit. Variables and nets may be explicitly defined by reg and wire declarations, respectively. Furthermore, all ports of a module also are nets or variables (if declared as reg variables) within that module. By default, outputs of a module are wire nets, unless explicitly declared as a reg variable. For example, in Figure 2.11(b), the output port *W* is a net that will be connected to the final output of the circuit.

Each port connection has a list of variables and nets in parentheses. Each variable or net in the list connects to a port of the module instance, according to the order of ports in the module instance's original module definition, referred to as an ***ordered port connection***. For example, module instance *And2_1* in Figure 2.11(d) is an *And2* module, which has ports *X, Y,* and *F.* The module instantiation statement "*And2 And2_1(K, P, N1);*" thus connects *(K, P, N1)* to *And2_1*'s ports *(X, Y, F)*. In other words, the statement connects *K* to *And2_1*'s *X* port, *P* to *And2_1*'s *Y* port, and *N1* to *And2_1*'s *F* port.

Example 2.2: Creating a circuit using module instantiations

This example creates a module for a 2x1 multiplexor, defining the mux's contents using a circuit. Figure 2.13(a) shows a block diagram for a 2x1 mux.

We'll follow the several-step procedure defined earlier:

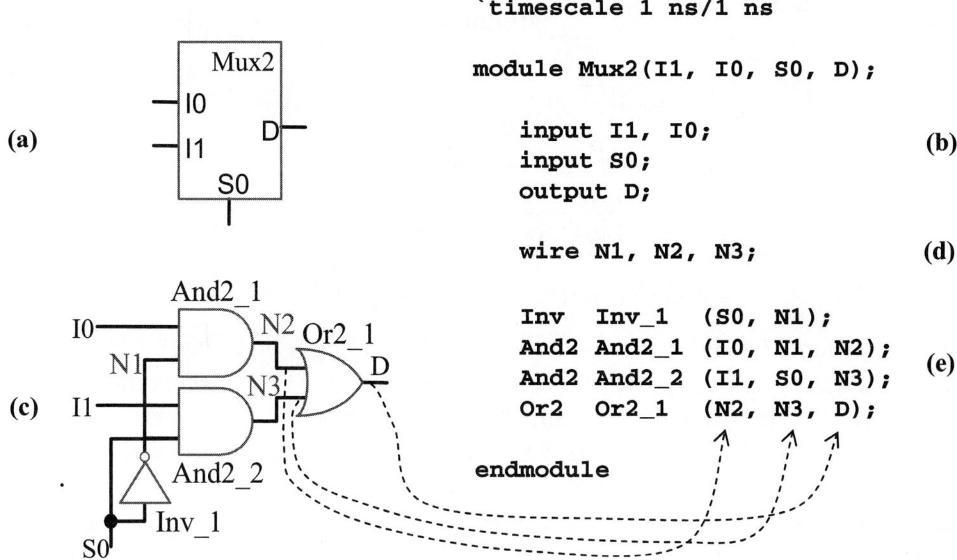

Figure 2.13 2x1 mux circuit example: (a) block diagram, (b) module definition start, (c) desired circuit with module instances and internal wires labeled, (d) declarations for internal wires, (e) module instantiation statements.

1. We begin a module definition for a 2x1 mux, using the proper inputs and outputs, as shown in Figure 2.13(b).
2. We define the internal wires, which we named *N1*, *N2*, and *N3*, as shown in Figure 2.13(d). Note that we should have sketched the circuit in Figure 2.13(c) in order to know how many internal wires will be needed.
3. Given the circuit in Figure 2.13(c), we instantiate modules and create connections using module instantiation statements as in Figure 2.13(e).

[SIMUL] SIMULATING THE CIRCUIT

Simulating a module whose contents are defined as a circuit is no different than simulating a module whose contents are defined as a procedure. We simply create a testbench that

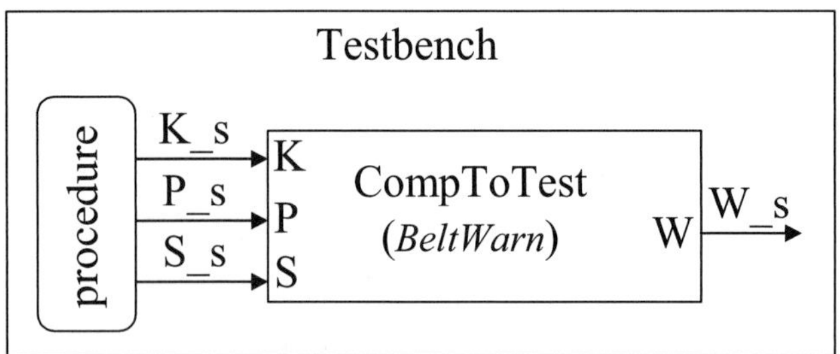

Figure 2.14 *BeltWarn* module's testbench setup.

instantiates the module, and that provides input values using a procedure, as was done in Section 2.1. Figure 2.14 shows the setup of a testbench for the *BeltWarn* module.

Figure 2.15 shows a testbench for the *BeltWarn* module. The testbench has a similar format to the testbench shown in Figure 2.8. Note several features of the standard testbench format. First, note that the testbench uses a module instantiation statement. Second, note that the testbench declares reg variables *K_s*, *P_s*, *S_s* for the module instances inputs *K*, *P*, and *S* and declares wire net *W_s* for output *W*. Reg variables were used so that we could assign values, which are held between assignments. Those items are needed because the procedure that follows *cannot* directly access the module instance's ports, whereas the procedure *can* access the declared variables and wires. We chose to append "*_s*" to the variable and net names to clearly distinguish them from the ports. Finally, note that a module can consist of both a module instantiation statement and a procedure statement. A module can be composed from any number of items, all of which behave as though they execute in parallel to jointly describe a module's overall behavior.

```
`timescale 1 ns/1 ns

module Testbench();

   reg K_s, P_s, S_s;
   wire W_s;

   BeltWarn CompToTest(K_s, P_s, S_s, W_s);

   initial begin
      K_s <= 0; P_s <= 0; S_s <= 0;
      #10 K_s <= 0; P_s <= 1; S_s <= 0;
      #10 K_s <= 1; P_s <= 1; S_s <= 0;
      #10 K_s <= 1; P_s <= 1; S_s <= 1;
   end

endmodule
```

Figure 2.15 Testbench for *BeltWarn* module.

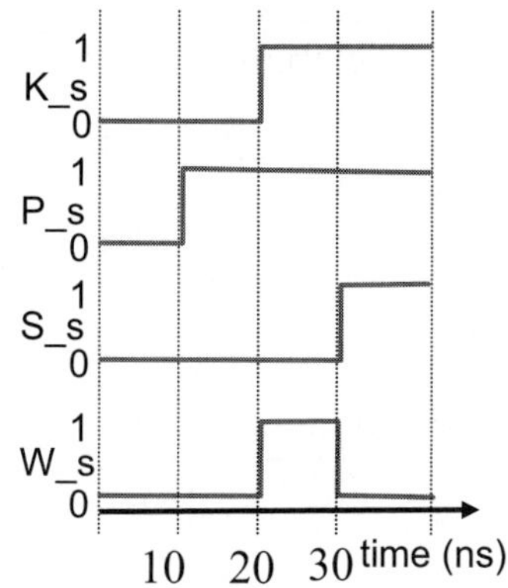

Figure 2.16 Waveforms generated by simulation of testbench for *BeltWarn*.

The testbench defines four test vectors, setting the *BeltWarn* instance's inputs *K*, *P*, and *S* to *000*, *010*, *110*, and *111*, holding each test vector for 10 nanoseconds of simulated time. Figure 2.16 shows the waveforms resulting from simulating the testbench.

Because the component has three binary inputs, the number of possible test vectors is $2^3 = 8$. A complete testbench would generate all eight such vectors. Creating a complete testbench becomes increasingly difficult for modules with more inputs, because the number of test vectors increases exponentially, requiring 2^n test vectors for a combinational circuit with n inputs. A testbench will thus typically only test a subset of all possible vectors.

2.3 TOP-DOWN DESIGN—COMBINATIONAL BEHAVIOR TO STRUCTURE

Early in the design process, a designer may know the behavior of a system, but may not yet have designed the structure. For example, for the *BeltWarn* example, a designer may know that the desired behavior is $W = KPS'$, but may not yet have designed the circuit shown in Figure 2.10(b). Designers therefore commonly follow a top-down design approach. In a ***top-down design approach***, illustrated in Figure 2.17, a designer first captures a system's behavior and simulates the system, and then creates the system's structure and simulates the system again. If the designer created the system structure correctly, then the behavior and structure simulations should yield identical waveforms. Following a top-down design process enables a designer to focus first on getting the behavior right, unfettered by the details of designing structure. The *BeltWarn* example is a small example — larger examples might have complex behavior that could be difficult to get right, making a top-down approach highly advantageous.

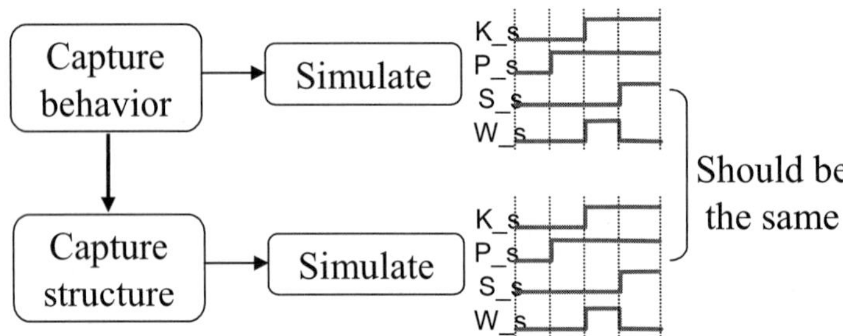

Figure 2.17 Top-down design process.

PROCEDURES WITH ASSIGNMENT STATEMENTS

A common way to describe a system's behavior is to use an always procedure. The simplest always procedure contains a single assignment statement. An always procedure describing the *BeltWarn* system's behavior appears in Figure 2.18. The procedure has an event control list with ports *K*, *P*, and *S* (i.e., is sensitive to *K*, *P*, and *S*), meaning the procedure executes whenever an event occurs (a value changes) on one of those ports. The procedure contains an assignment that sets output port *W* to the appropriate value. The testbench for this module would be the same testbench as appears in Figure 2.15, with no modifications. Simulat-

```
`timescale 1 ns/1 ns

module BeltWarn(K, P, S, W);

   input K, P, S;
   output W;
   reg W;

   always @(K, P, S) begin
      W <= K & P & ~S;
   end
endmodule
```

Figure 2.18 *BeltWarn* behavior described using an always procedure with a single assignment statement.

ing that testbench would result in the waveforms of Figure 2.16. Following a top-down design approach, a designer might then create the circuit shown in Figure 2.10(b), and simulate the system again using the same testbench, resulting in the same waveforms. An ***assignment statement*** assigns a value to a variable. The left side of the assignment operator "<=" must be a variable (i.e., it may not be a net). The right side may be an expression involving operators. ***Built-in bitwise operators*** include **&** (AND), | (OR), ~ (NOT), ^ (XOR), and ~^ (XNOR). As an example, consider creating a procedure to compute *F= C'H + CH'*. The procedure would be defined with event control having events *C* and *H* as follows: "*always @(C,H)* begin". The procedure could then contain the assignment statement: "*F <= (~C&H) | (C&~H);*". Alternatively, the procedure could contain the assignment statement: "*F <= C ^ H;*".

Note that a procedure may have more than one assignment statement. Figure 2.19 shows a procedure having two assignment statements.

PROCEDURES WITH IF-ELSE STATEMENTS

In addition to having an assignment statement, a procedure may have other kinds of statements, such as an if-else statement. An ***if-else statement*** (also known as a ***conditional statement***) starts with "*if (expression)*". If the expression evaluates to true, then the statement that follows is executed. For example, Figure 2.20 shows behavior for the *BeltWarn* example using a procedure having an *if-else* statement. If the expression *(K & P & ~S)* evaluates to true, the statement "*W <= 1;*" executes. If the expression instead evaluates to false, the

```
`timescale 1 ns/1 ns

module TwoOutputEx(A, B, C, F, G);

   input A, B, C;
   output F, G;
   reg F, G;

   always @(A, B, C) begin
      F <= (B & B) | ~C;
      G <= (A & B) | (B & C);
   end
endmodule
```

Figure 2.19 Two assignment statements in a procedure.

```
`timescale 1 ns/1 ns

module BeltWarn(K, P, S, W);

   input K, P, S;
   output W;
   reg W;

   always @(K, P, S) begin
      if ((K & P & ~S) == 1)
         W <= 1;
      else
         W <= 0;
   end
endmodule
```

Figure 2.20 *BeltWarn* behavior described using a procedure having an if-else statement.

"*W* <= *1;*" statement is skipped, and instead the statement following the *else* keyword is executed, namely "*W* <= *0;*". The *else* part of an *if-else* statement is optional.

To say that an expression evaluates to ***true*** means that the expression evaluates to any non-zero value. For clarity, we explicitly compared the result of *(K & P & ~S)* to *1*, although the comparison with *1* wasn't strictly necessary. Such explicit comparison is good practice for readability. "==" is the built-in ***logical equality operator***, which compares two items for equality, returning *1* if equal, and *0* if not equal.

Often multiple possibilities, not just the two possibilities considered in an *if-else* statement, must be represented. Multiple possibilities can be described by stringing *if-else* statements together. Such a description is common enough to be known separately as an ***if-else-if*** construct, even though the construct is not actually a distinct language construct. Figure 2.21(a) shows a procedure having an *if-else-if* construct, formed from three *if-else* statements strung together, describing the behavior of a 4x1 multiplexor. The figure shows which particular statements would be executed if the procedure were executed with *S1S0=01*. The first expression evaluates to false, so its statement "*D* <= *I0;*" would be skipped, and the first *else*'s statement would execute. That statement is another *if-else* statement, whose expression evaluates to true, so its statement "*D* <= *I1;*" would execute. The remaining parts of the *if-else-if* construct would be skipped.

Figure 2.21(b) shows the same *if-else-if* construct using non-standard indentation that shows how the three *if-else* statements are nested, which clearly shows why remaining parts of the construct are skipped as soon as an expression evaluates to true.

Figure 2.21 uses the following expression in the if statement: "*if (S1==0 && S0==0)*". "&&" is the logical AND operator. When dealing with bit operands, the earlier-defined bit-

```
`timescale 1 ns/1 ns

module Mux4(I3, I2, I1, I0, S1, S0, D);

   input I3, I2, I1, I0;
   input S1, S0;
   output D;
   reg D;

   always @(I3, I2, I1, I0, S1, S0)
   begin
      if (S1==0 && S0==0)
         D <= I0;
      else if (S1==0 && S0==1)
         D <= I1;
      else if (S1==1 && S0==0)
         D <= I2;
      else
         D <= I3;
   end
endmodule
```

(a)

(b)

```
if (S1==0 && S0==0)
   D <= I0;
else
   if (S1==0 && S0==1)
      D <= I1;
   else
      if (S1==1 && S0==0)
         D <= I2;
      else
         D <= I3;
```

Figure 2.21 4x1 mux: (a) described using a procedure using an if-else-if construct, and showing statement executed if S1S0=01, (b) equivalent if-else-if construct using non-standard indentation that shows the nesting of the three if-else statements.

wise AND operator "&" and the logical AND operator "&&" behave similarly. Their distinction will be discussed later.

Example 2.3: 2x4 decoder

This example describes a 2x4 decoder's behavior using a procedure having an if-else-if construct. The module definition appears in Figure 2.22, having inputs *I1* and *I0*. The module's content has a procedure that is sensitive to inputs *I1* and *I0*.

The procedure contains an if-else-if statement whose four parts detect each of the four possible conditions of *i1i0* = *00*, *01*, *10*, or *11*.

This example illustrates how to execute multiple statements, rather than just one statement, when an expression is true. To do so, one merely encloses those statements within the keywords *begin* and *end*. Those keywords and the enclosed statements are collectively known as a ***begin-end block***, also called a ***sequential block***. Note that the procedure itself contains a begin-end block too.

Note that two (or more) assignment statements (or other types of statements) may appear on a single line. New lines and extra spaces have no impact other than enhancing readability of the code.

```
`timescale 1 ns/1 ns

module Dcd2x4(I1, I0, D3, D2, D1, D0);

   input I1, I0;
   output D3, D2, D1, D0;
   reg D3, D2, D1, D0;

   always @(I1, I0)
   begin
      if (I1==0 && I0==0)
      begin
         D3 <= 0; D2 <= 0;
         D1 <= 0; D0 <= 1;
      end
      else if (I1==0 && I0==1)
      begin
         D3 <= 0; D2 <= 0;
         D1 <= 1; D0 <= 0;
      end
      else if (I1==1 && I0==0)
      begin
         D3 <= 0; D2 <= 1;
         D1 <= 0; D0 <= 0;
      end
      else
      begin
         D3 <= 1; D2 <= 0;
         D1 <= 0; D0 <= 0;
      end
   end
endmodule
```

Figure 2.22 2x4 decoder described using a procedure having an *if-else-if* construct

Furthermore, note that the order of assignment statements using "<=" within a begin-end block does not matter in this case.

■

MULTIPLE MODULE DESCRIPTIONS FOR ONE MODULE

A top-down design process involves capturing two descriptions for the same module—first a behavioral description, and then a structural description. Fortunately, the first module need not be deleted in order to capture the second module. Instead, the modules can be saved in different files. For example, Figure 2.23 shows two *BeltWarn* module descriptions, one behavioral, the other structural. A designer might first capture the behavioral module, saved perhaps in a file called *vldd_ch2_BeltWarnBeh.v,* and simulate using the testbench in Figure 2.15. The designer might then copy that file to another file called

```
`timescale 1 ns/1 ns

module BeltWarn(K, P, S, W);

   input K, P, S;
   output W;
   reg W;

   always @(K, P, S) begin
      W <= K & P & ~S;
   end
endmodule
```

(a)

```
`timescale 1 ns/1 ns

module BeltWarn(K, P, S, W);

   input K, P, S;
   output W;

   wire N1, N2;

   And2 And2_1(K, P, N1);
   Inv  Inv_1(S, N2);
   And2 And2_2(N1, N2, W);

endmodule
```

(b)

Figure 2.23 Two *BeltWarn* modules: (a) behavioral, (b) structural. Each can be saved in a separate file.

vldd_ch2_BeltWarnStruct.v, and while preserving the module definition start that lists the ports, might then replace the remaining part by the structural description.

During simulation, only one module can be used. Simulators provide simple mechanisms for selecting which module file to use.

COMMON PITFALLS

Certain mistakes are made frequently. Such mistakes are known as ***common pitfalls***. We describe a few common pitfalls that occur when describing combinational behavior using a procedure. Recall that for combinational behavior, the output value is purely a function of the present input values, whereas for sequential behavior, the output value is a function of present and past input values, i.e., sequential behavior has memory.

Missing inputs from event control expression

When using an always procedure to describe combinational behavior, one common pitfall is to not include all the module's inputs in the procedure's event control expression. Figure 2.24(a) provides an example of this mistake in an always procedure that was intended to describe a 4x1 mux. The procedure's event control expression is missing inputs *I3*, *I2*, *I1*, and *I0*. That omission results in a module whose behavior does not correspond to a 4x1 mux. Figure 2.24(b) illustrates the incorrect behavior. Suppose initially that *S1S0=01*, so *D=I1*, and *I1* happens to be *0*. If *S1* or *S0* changes, the procedure will execute, and recompute the correct value of the output *D*. In the figure, when *S1* changes to *1*, the procedure executes and sets *D=I3*, and *I3* happens to be *1*. However, if *I3*, *I2*, *I1*, or *I0* changes, the procedure will not execute, because they are not in the event control expression. In the figure, *I3* changes from *1* to *0*, but the module continues to output the old value of *1*, because the procedure did not execute when *I3* changed. Instead, the procedure should have again

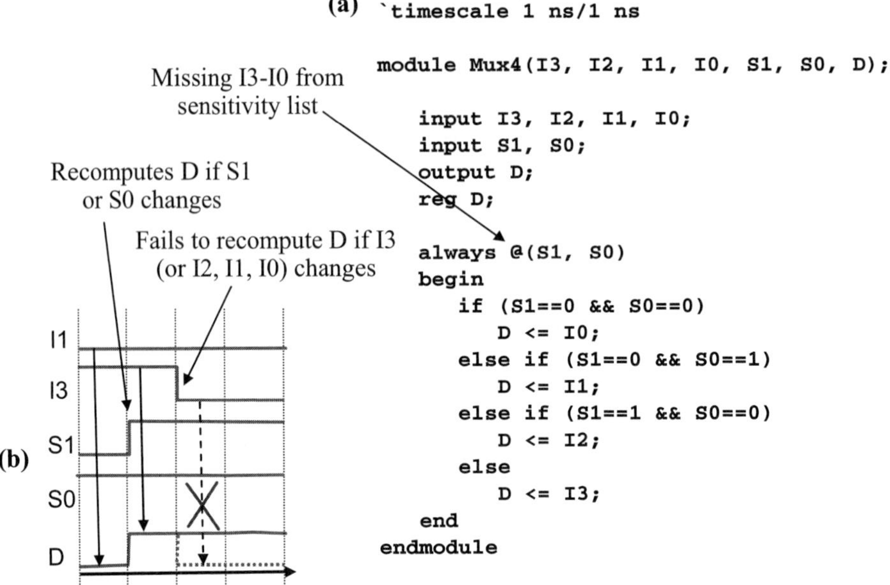

(a)
`timescale 1 ns/1 ns
module Mux4(I3, I2, I1, I0, S1, S0, D);
input I3, I2, I1, I0;
input S1, S0;
output D;
reg D;
always @(S1, S0)
begin
if (S1==0 && S0==0)
D <= I0;
else if (S1==0 && S0==1)
D <= I1;
else if (S1==1 && S0==0)
D <= I2;
else
D <= I3;
end
endmodule
Missing I3-I0 from sensitivity list
Recomputes D if S1 or S0 changes
Fails to recompute D if I3 (or I2, I1, I0) changes
(b)
I1
I3
S1
S0
D

Figure 2.24 Incorrect description of a 4x1 mux: (a) event control sensitivity list with missing inputs, (b) undesired behavior that appears during simulation.

executed, and set *D=I3*, meaning *0*. Hence, the behavior has some form of memory, and is therefore sequential.

Note that this mistake is not a Verilog error. The code is legal Verilog. The code just does not describe a 4x1 mux.

Verilog provides a mechanism to help avoid this pitfall. The event control may be listed as "@*", known as an implicit event control expression (or *implicit sensitivity list*), which automatically adds all nets and variables that are read by the controlled statement (or statement group) to the event control expression. Thus, starting the mux procedure as: "*always @* begin*", would have been equivalent to starting the procedure as "*always @(S1,S0,I0,I1,I2,I3) begin*". "*@(*)*" is also equivalent to "@*".

Outputs not assigned on every pass

When using an always procedure to describe combinational behavior, another common pitfall is to fail to assign every output on every possible pass through the procedure. Figure 2.25(a) provides an example of that mistake in a procedure that was intended to describe a 2x4 decoder. The last *else if* part is missing assignments to *D2*, *D1*, and *D0*.

The omission results in a procedure whose behavior does not correspond to a 2x4 decoder. Figure 2.25(b) illustrates the incorrect behavior. Suppose initially that *I1I0=10*. Therefore, the output *D2* is *1,* and all other outputs are *0*. Suppose then that *I1I0* changes to *11* as shown. The procedure will execute, and the last *else if* part will execute. However, that last *else if* only has the statement "*D3 <= 1;*". Thus, *D3* will be updated to *1* as shown

(a)

```
`timescale 1 ns/1 ns

module Dcd2x4(I1, I0, D3, D2, D1, D0);

   input I1, I0;
   output D3, D2, D1, D0;
   reg D3, D2, D1, D0;

   always @(I1, I0)
   begin
      if (I1==0 && I0==0)
      begin
         D3 <= 0; D2 <= 0;
         D1 <= 0; D0 <= 1;
      end
      else if (I1==0 && I0==1)
      begin
         D3 <= 0; D2 <= 0;
         D1 <= 1; D0 <= 0;
      end
      else if (I1==1 && I0==0)
      begin
         D3 <= 0; D2 <= 1;
         D1 <= 0; D0 <= 0;
      end
      else if (I1==1 && I0==1)
      begin
         D3 <= 1;
      end
      // Note: missing assignments
      // to every output in last "else if"
   end
endmodule
```

(b)

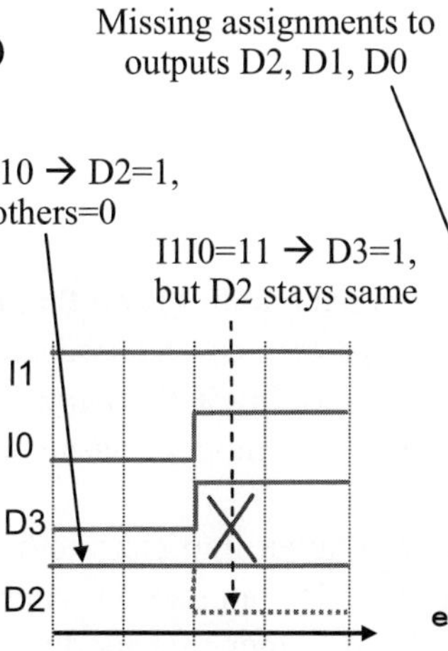

Missing assignments to outputs D2, D1, D0

I1I0=10 → D2=1, others=0

I1I0=11 → D3=1, but D2 stays same

I1

I0

D3

D2

Figure 2.25 Incorrect 2x4 decoder description: (a) some outputs not assigned on every pass, (b) incorrect behavior that appears during simulation.

in Figure 2.25(b), but *D2* will also remain at *1* because it won't be explicitly set to *0* in that last *else if* part. Hence, the circuit has some form of memory, and is therefore sequential.

Note that this mistake is not a Verilog error. The code is legal Verilog. The code just does not describe a 2x4 decoder.

The same pitfall occurs when not all input combinations are included in an *if-else-if* construct. For example, a designer might forget to include the last *else if* part entirely, thus not including the input combination *I1I0=11* in the *if-else-if* construct. If *I1* or *I0* changes such that *I1I0=11*, the procedure would execute, but would reach the end of the procedure without executing any assignment statements. Thus, the output would remember the previous value, and hence the procedure would not describe a 2x4 decoder. This pitfall results in what is commonly referred to as an ***inferred latch***, because the procedure describes a circuit that must include a latch or some other form of memory (more on inferred latches later).

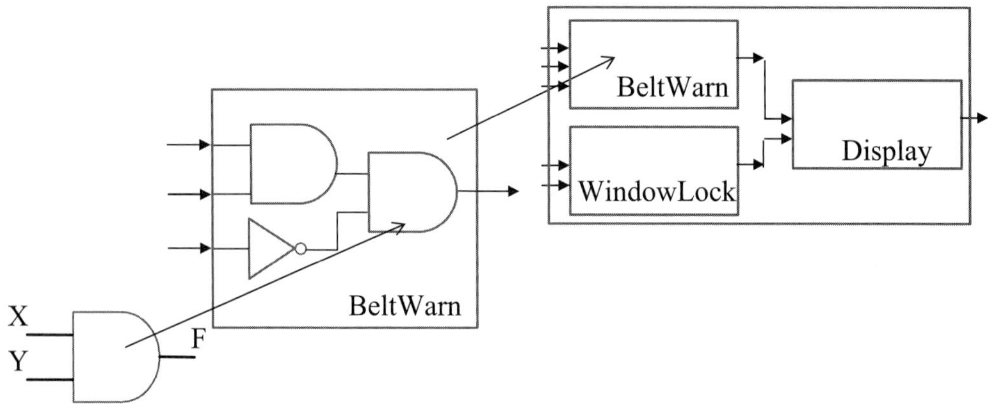

Figure 2.26 Hierarchy is a powerful mechanism for managing complexity.

2.4 HIERARCHICAL CIRCUITS

After creating a module (behaviorally or structurally), we may want to use that module as an instance in another design. We did this earlier when we created an *And2* module, and then used that *And2* module as an instance in a circuit describing a *BeltWarn* module, as shown in Figure 2.26. Likewise, we could use the *BeltWarn* module as an instance in another module, as shown in the figure.

Hierarchy is the notion that a module may be broken down into sub-modules, where each sub-module itself may be broken down into sub-modules, and so on. Hierarchy is a powerful mechanism for managing complexity, since the designer of a module need only think of a smaller number of sub-modules one level down, rather than having to think of a larger numbers of sub-modules at the bottom level.

USING MODULES AS INSTANCES

Verilog directly supports hierarchy by allowing a module to be used as a module instance in another module. We will demonstrate such hierarchy using an example.

Example 2.4: 4-bit 2x1 mux

Consider the design of a 4-bit 2x1 mux. We begin by first designing a 2x1 mux module as a circuit built from gate-level instances, as was done in Figure 2.13. Next, we design a 4-bit 2x1 mux as a circuit built from 2x1 mux instances, as shown in Figure 2.27. The 4-bit 2x1 mux could then be used as an instance in some other design, and so on.

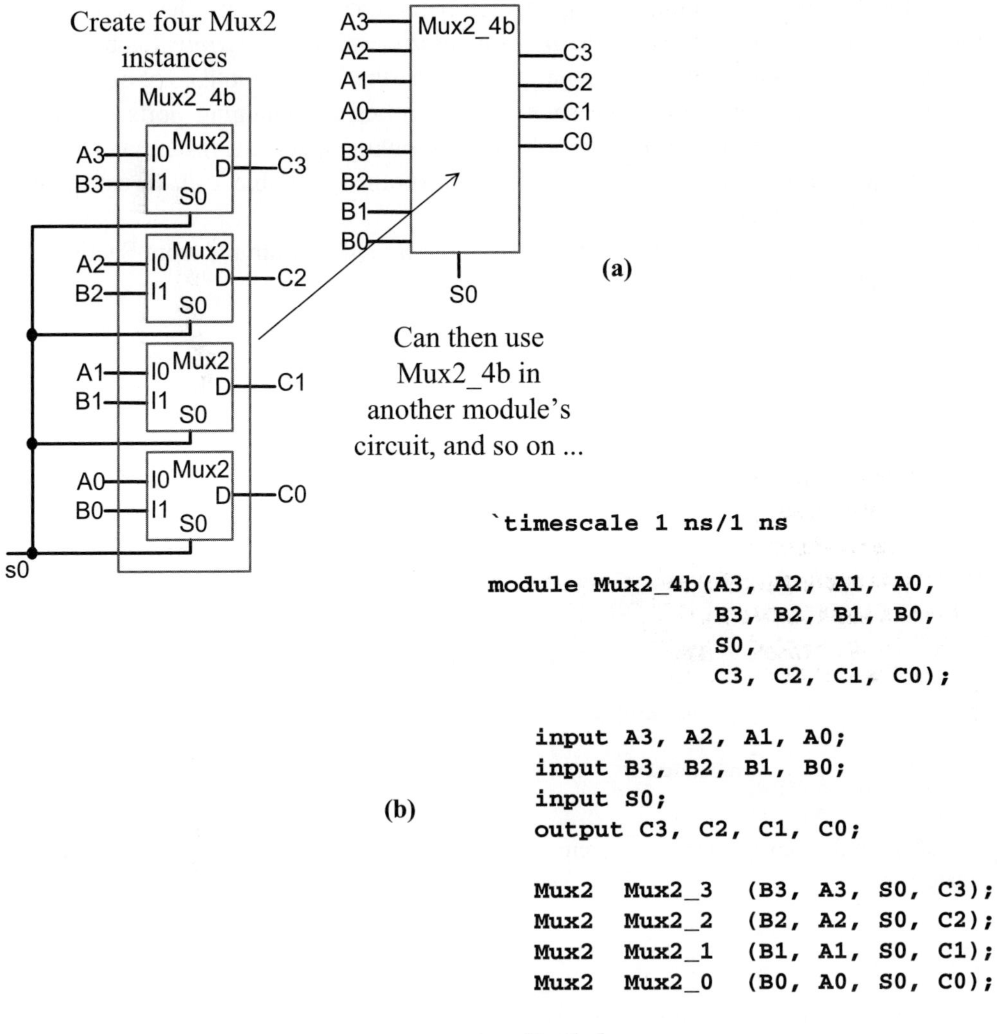


```
`timescale 1 ns/1 ns

module Mux2_4b(A3, A2, A1, A0,
               B3, B2, B1, B0,
               S0,
               C3, C2, C1, C0);

   input A3, A2, A1, A0;
   input B3, B2, B1, B0;
   input S0;
   output C3, C2, C1, C0;

   Mux2  Mux2_3  (B3, A3, S0, C3);
   Mux2  Mux2_2  (B2, A2, S0, C2);
   Mux2  Mux2_1  (B1, A1, S0, C1);
   Mux2  Mux2_0  (B0, A0, S0, C0);

endmodule
```

Figure 2.27 Using hierarchy: (a) to build a 4-bit 2x1 mux from 2x1 muxes, (b) Verilog description.

2.5 BUILT-IN LOGIC GATES

We previously defined modules for AND, OR, and NOT gates. However, Verilog has several ***built-in gates*** that can be instantiated, thus relieving the designer from having to define gate modules. The built-in gates include ***and***, ***or***, ***nand***, ***nor***, ***xor***, and ***xnor***. Each gate has one output, and one or more inputs. The output is always the first port in the list of port connections in a module instantiation statement. The number of remaining ports in the list determines the size of the gate. For example, the following statement instantiates a four-input AND gate: "*and a1(out, in1, in2, in3, in4);*". Another available built-in gate is ***not***, which has exactly one input.

A description using the built-in gates to design the *BeltWarn* example from Section 2.2 is shown in Figure 2.28.

```
`timescale 1 ns/1 ns

module BeltWarn(K, P, S, W);

   input K, P, S;
   output W;

   wire N1, N2;

   and And_1(N1, K, P);
   not Inv_1(N2, S);
   and And_2(W, N1, N2);

endmodule
```

Figure 2.28 Module contents defined as a circuit for the *BeltWarn* module, using Verilog's built-in logic gates.

CHAPTER 3

Sequential Logic Design

3.1 REGISTER BEHAVIOR

Sequential circuits store bits. A basic storage component is a register. A basic N-bit register can store N bits. Figure 3.1 illustrates a 4-bit register. That register has a clock input, a reset input (*Rst*), four data inputs (*I3*, *I2*, *I1*, *I0*), and four data outputs (*Q3*, *Q2*, *Q1*, *Q0*). The register shown is loaded with its data inputs on every clock cycle. One approach to describing a 4-bit register is structurally, using 4 D flip-flops. However, another approach to describing a 4-bit register is behaviorally, an approach we now introduce.

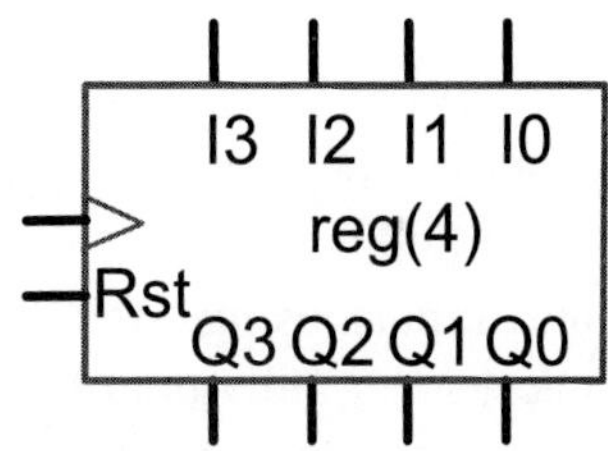

Figure 3.1 4-bit register.

VECTORS

Figure 3.2 shows a behavioral description of a 4-bit register. Briefly, the description consists of a single always procedure that stores a new value into the 4-bit variable *Q* on every rising clock edge. If the reset input was *1* during that clock edge, the register stores "*0000*". Otherwise, the register stores into *Q* whatever values are on the 4-bit input *I*. We now explain various aspects of the register's description in more detail.

The module could have declared four 1-bit ports for the four data inputs *I3*, *I2*, *I1*, *I0*, as shown in Figure 3.3(a). Instead, the module declares one 4-bit port, *I*, by declaring *I* as "*input [3:0] I;*", as in Figure 3.3(b). A ***vector*** data type defines a collection of bits, and is more convenient than declaring each bit separately. The vector declaration must specify the numbering and order of the bits using a ***range specification***, defined here as *[3:0]*. The *[3:0]* part also defines how many bits exist. In this example, *[3:0]* means the bits are num-

```
`timescale 1 ns/1 ns

module Reg4(I, Q, Clk, Rst);

   input [3:0] I;
   output [3:0] Q;
   reg [3:0] Q;
   input Clk, Rst;

   always @(posedge Clk) begin
      if (Rst == 1 )
         Q <= 4'b0000;
      else
         Q <= I;
   end
endmodule
```

Figure 3.2 4-bit register description.

bered 3, 2, 1, 0, and thus there are four bits, as illustrated in Figure 3.3(b). We could have numbered the bits *[0:3]*, or even *[1:4]*, but convention usually puts the highest-order bit on the left and numbering typically begins at 0. Figure 3.2 declares the data outputs similarly to the data inputs, using one 4-bit port *Q* of vector type.

To access an individual bit of a vector, we use a a ***bit selection*** by specifying the bit position in brackets, e.g., *Q[2] <= I[1]* would assign input bit 1 to output bit 2. The benefit of using a vector becomes evident when assigning multiple bits. For example, note in the description that, at one point, *Q* gets assigned to *I* using the statement "*Q <= I;*". That single statement actually represents four assignments: *Q[3] <= I[3]*, *Q[2] <= I[2]*, *Q[1] <= I[1]*, and *Q[0] <= I[0]*. As another example, note in the description that all four bits of *Q* are set to *0*s with one statement: "*Q <= 4'b0000;*".

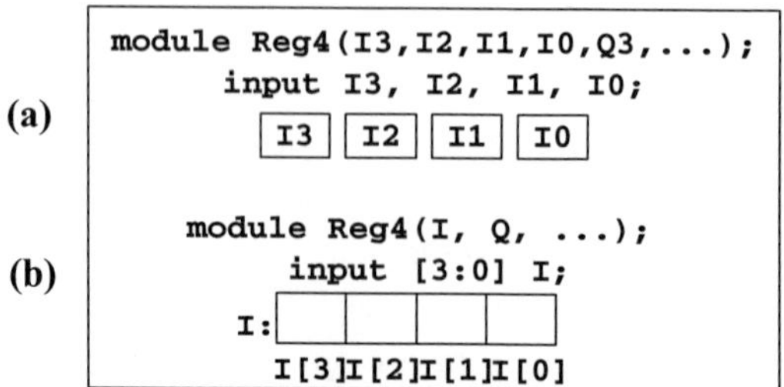

Figure 3.3. Two ways of declaring a 4-bit input: (a) as four bits, (b) as a 4-bit vector.

CONSTANT NUMBERS

4'b0000, which appears in Figure 3.2, is the way to represent a 4-bit based constant number value consisting of all *0*s. *4* is the size (in number of bits), *b*, or *B*, means the base in binary, and *0000* is the binary value. Similarly, *4'b0101* would specify a 4-bit number corresponding to the binary value *0101*, or decimal value of 5. Other bases for constants are decimal (*d* or *D*), octal (*o* or *O*), and hexadecimal (*h* or *H*). For example, *12'hFA2* would specify a 12-bit hexadecimal number (3 hex digits requires 12 bits) with the hex value being *FA2*. The size part is always in bits, and is optional (e.g., *'hFA2* is acceptable). For decimal numbers, the base part is also optional, e.g., either *8'd255* or just *255* are acceptable. Thus, note that in our number usage in earlier chapters, such as the usage in the statement "*A <= 1;*", *1* and *0* actually represent decimal numbers. *'b1* and *'b0* would explicitly represent bits. Underscores may be inserted into a constant number for readability, such as *12'b1111_1010_0010* or *8_000_000*. Constant numbers of any of the above bases are known as integer constants.

SYNCHRONOUS STORAGE USING A REG VARIABLE

The register's description in Figure 3.2 has a single procedure whose event control involves only the clock input. Unlike a combinational circuit, a register's data outputs are not affected immediately by changes on the register's data inputs; instead, only on a rising clock edge does the register load the data inputs. Thus, the register description's procedure event control only involves the clock input *Clk*. Furthermore, the event control expression specifies the event as "*posedge Clk*", meaning that only a positive edge event on *Clk* should cause the procedure to execute. ***posedge*** is a positive edge event, also known as a ***rising edge***, which is a transition from *0* to *1*. (If the event control were only "*Clk*", then any change on *Clk*, such as *0* to *1*, or *1* to *0*, would cause the procedure to execute). A negative edge event, ***negedge***, also exists in the language. In practice, most registers are positive edge triggered.

Upon execution, the procedure checks if the reset input, *Rst*, is *1*. If so, the register should be cleared to *0*s, and the procedure does so with the statement "*Q <= 4'b0000;*". If *Rst* was not *1*, then the register should load the data inputs, which the procedure does using the statement "*Q <= I;*". Notice that the register's contents will only be reset to all *0*s upon a rising clock edge when the *Rst* input is *1*. Thus, resetting the contents of the register to all *0*s will be synchronized with a rising clock edge. A reset synchronized with a clock edge is called a ***synchronous reset***. An alternative reset implementation is an asynchronous reset, which will be described later in this chapter.

The register's storage is achieved by writing to *Q*. Because output port *Q* was also declared to be a reg variable, and because reg variables store their value between assignments, then *Q* implements the register's storage. *Q* will maintain its previously-written value until the next write to *Q*, thus achieving the desired storage of the register.

[SIMUL] TESTBENCHES WITH CLOCKS

A testbench for a register component, illustrated in Figure 3.4, has a no-port module definition with reg and wire declarations and a module instantiation, all being similar to those of previously introduced testbenches. However, the register's testbench has two procedures, rather than just one procedure as in previous testbenches.

The first procedure, named in a comment as *Clock Procedure*, generates values for the clock, with the clock having a 20 ns period. The procedure sets the clock to *0* for 10 ns, and then sets the clock to *1* for 10 ns. Being an always procedure, the procedure repeats itself, meaning the procedure sets the clock to *0* again for 10 ns, then to *1* again for 10 ns, and so on.

The second procedure, named in a comment as *Vector Procedure*, serves the purpose seen in previous testbenches, namely of generating an instance's input test vectors.

```
`timescale 1 ns/1 ns

module Testbench();

   reg [3:0] I_s;
   reg Clk_s, Rst_s;
   wire [3:0] Q_s;

   Reg4 CompToTest(I_s, Q_s, Clk_s, Rst_s);

   // Clock Procedure
   always begin
      Clk_s <= 0;
      #10;
      Clk_s <= 1;
      #10;
   end   // Note: Procedure repeats

   // Vector Procedure
   initial begin
      Rst_s <= 1;
      I_s <= 4'b0000;
      @(posedge Clk_s);
      #5 Rst_s <= 0;
      I_s <= 4'b0000;
      @(posedge Clk_s);
      #5 Rst_s <= 0;
      I_s <= 4'b1010;
      @(posedge Clk_s);
      #5 Rst_s <= 0;
      I_s <= 4'b1111;
   end
endmodule
```

Figure 3.4 Register testbench.

Notice in this example that two procedures may access the same variable. The clock variable *Clk_s* is accessed by the clock procedure and also by the vector procedure. For our purposes, only one always procedure should ever *assign* a particular variable. If multiple procedures assign the same variable, what is known as a simulation ***race condition*** may exist, meaning that two simulators may generate different output results depending on what order they execute the procedures. Such legal variation in simulation output is known as ***non-deterministic*** behavior, and is usually something we wish to avoid. (Actually, multiple procedures could assign a single variable in a deterministic way in certain situations; this subject will be discussed in Section 4.5. In Figure 3.4, the clock procedure writes the variable *Clk_s*, while the vector procedure reads the variable. Multiple procedures may read a single variable.

The vector procedure in Figure 3.4 begins by resetting the register using "*Rst_s <= 1;*". Note that the procedure also sets *I_s* to "*0000*", even though such setting of *I_s* is really not necessary because the register internally sets itself to "*0000*" upon a reset. However, good practice dictates setting all of an instance's inputs to some defined value at the beginning of a testbench's vector procedure, even if those values are not used. Such setting prevents the potential problem of forgetting to set a particular input value later in the vector procedure, which could lead to incorrect simulation results or unexpected behavior.

The vector procedure consists of four test vectors. The first vector resets the register, as discussed above. The second vector loads the register with "*0000*". The third vector loads "*1010*", and the fourth vector loads "*1111*". The first three vectors are followed by a statement "*@(posedge Clk_s);*". Such event control may be prepended to a statement in order to synchronize that statement's execution with an event. In this case, the event control precedes a ***null*** statement, which is a statement consisting of nothing but a semicolon. Previous examples of event control were prepended to a sequential block statement (a begin-end block). The event control in the testbench has the effect of causing the procedure to wait until the next rising clock edge before proceeding with the next test vector.

Before setting the register's inputs with the next vector, the procedure delays for 5 ns. That extra delay seeks to make the simulation waveforms easier to read, by having the newly-loaded values appear separately from the next vectors, which appear 5 ns later.

Figure 3.5 shows waveforms that would be generated by the testbench of Figure 3.4. *Clk_s* alternates between *1* and *0* every 10 ns. *Rst_s* is initially *1*. Thus, when the first rising clock edge appears at time 10 ns, the register's output *Q* (connected in the testbench to the net *Q_s*, which appears in the waveforms) resets to "*0000*". Note that before time 10 ns, *Q*'s value was unknown, indicated in the waveform as "*xxxx*", because no value had yet been written to *Q*. A bit's initial value is the unknown value *x*. *Rst_s* becomes *0* 5 ns later, at time 15 ns. *I* (connected to variable *I_s*, which appears in the waveform) is also set to "*0000*" at that time, but since *I* was earlier set to "*0000*", no change appears in *I*'s waveform. When the next rising clock edge appears, at time 30 ns, the register's output *Q* takes on the value on input *I*, which is "*0000*". *I* changes to "*1010*" 5 ns later. When the next rising clock edge

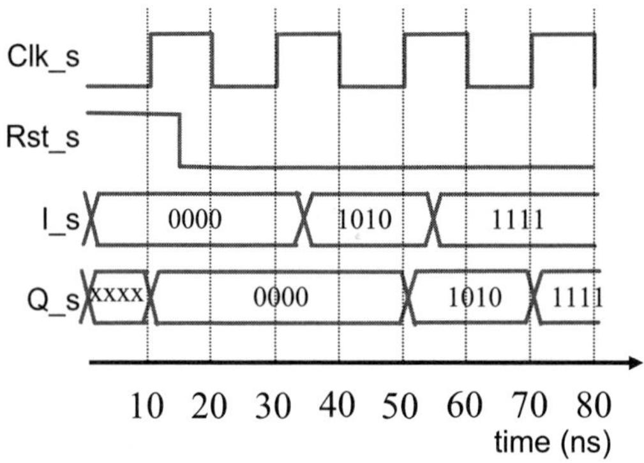

Figure 3.5 Register testbench waveforms.

appears, at time 50 ns, Q becomes "*1010*". The waveforms show that the register correctly loads its input I to its output Q only on rising clock edges.

[SIMUL] COMMON PITFALLS

Some common pitfalls exist when creating testbenches, which we now describe.

Using an always procedure instead of an initial procedure

A common pitfall is the use of an always procedure rather than an initial procedure for the test vector procedure, as shown in Figure 3.6. Repeated execution is typically not what was intended by the person who wrote the vector procedure.

Not including any delay control or event control in an always procedure

Another common pitfall is to not include any delay control or event control in an always procedure, as illustrated in Figure 3.7. The failure to include at least one delay or event control causes an infinite loop in a simulator. This pitfall is commonly encountered not just in testbench procedures, but in other procedures, too. For example, a mistake is to forget to include event control for an always procedure that is supposed to describe combinational

```
// Vector Procedure
always begin
   Rst_s <= 1;
   I_s <= 4'b0000;
   @(posedge Clk_s);
   ...
   @(posedge Clk_s);
   #5 Rst_s <= 0;
   I_s <= 4'b1111;
end
```

Figure 3.6 Common pitfall: Using an always procedure instead of an initial procedure.

```
// Vector Procedure
always begin
   Rst_s <= 1;
   I_s <= 4'b0000;
end
```

Figure 3.7 Common pitfall: Not including any delay control or event control in an always procedure.

logic. Although always procedures model concurrently-executing hardware components, a simulator executes each procedure one at a time, possibly executing each procedure up to the procedure's next delay or event control before moving on to execute the next procedure. When the simulator has executed every procedure (that needs to be executed) once, the simulator updates the simulator's generated waveforms, and re-executes procedures again. If a procedure has no delay or event control, then the simulator can never move on to the next procedure or update the simulator's waveforms. Instead, the simulator gets stuck in an infinite loop that repeatedly executes the statements of that procedure. The simulator appears to just "hang" and do nothing, as shown in Figure 3.8. In fact, the simulator is doing plenty of work, but that work consists of repeatedly executing one procedure over and over again.

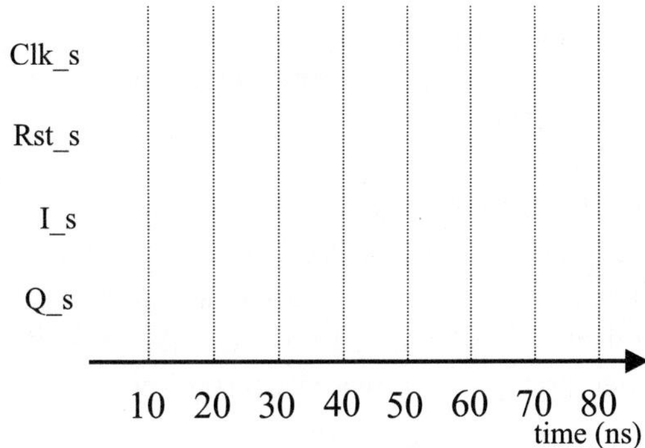

Figure 3.8 Common pitfall: Not including any delay or event control in an always procedure results in the simulator not generating any waveforms, instead appearing to just "hang."

Not initializing all input ports

A common pitfall is to forget to explicitly assign a value to every input port of a module instance being tested, as shown in Figure 3.9. A simulator will usually show such an un-initialized values by placing a "*x*" in the waveform of a bit data type, or placing nothing in the waveform of a different data type. While an unknown module input usually results in an unknown module output value, which is easy to detect by a designer, an unknown module input can sometimes result in a valid module output, depending on how the module's contents were written. In that case, the valid output may not be what the designer expects, and tracing the problem back to an un-initialized input can be difficult, especially when there

```
// Vector Procedure
always begin
   Rst_s <= 1;
   I_s <= 4'b0000;
   @(posedge Clk_s);
   ...
   @(posedge Clk_s);
   #5 Rst_s <= 0;
   I_s <= 4'b1111;
end
```

Figure 3.9 Common pitfall: Not initializing all input ports.

are many inputs or when the unknown input's waveform was not selected to be shown in the simulation output.

An even worse problem occurs if the simulator assigns a default value (like 0 or 1) to every variable. Simulators are not supposed to do that, but not all simulators are perfectly compliant. The problem is that a testbench and design may simulate correctly under one simulator, but when that same testbench and design are run (perhaps years later) on another simulator that does not assign a default value, they may fail to simulate properly.

Therefore, when creating a testbench procedure, some experienced designers will immediately write statements that initialize all of a module instance's inputs, setting those inputs to *0*s, *1*s, or whatever is appropriate, before beginning to write the procedure's test vectors.

Not declaring an identifier used in a port connection

Forgetting to explicitly declare an identifier used in a port connection can yield strange simulation behavior, for the following reason. Rather than treating such an omission as an error, Verilog implicitly declares the identifier as a net of the default net type, which is typically a 1-bit wire. Such a declaration is known as an ***implicit declaration***, intended to be a shortcut that reduces the amount of typing required for large netlists. Thus, the omission is not an error and may not even yield a warning message during compilation. The implicit declaration works fine if the identifier is supposed to be a 1-bit wire. But suppose that the declaration "*wire [3:0] Q_s;*" was omitted from Figure 3.4. Since *Q_s* is used in a port connection, it would be implicitly declared as a 1-bit wire, but it should have been a 4-bit wire. A warning message might appear during simulation, but could easily be overlooked. Verilog has many automatic conversion rules, which may convert the 4-bit value to a 1-bit value (obviously losing information), yielding unexpected simulation results. Explicitly declaring all wires and avoiding the use of implicit declarations may help to avoid this pitfall.

3.2 FINITE-STATE MACHINES (FSMS)—SEQUENTIAL BEHAVIOR

Finite-state machines (FSMs) are a standard way to describe the desired behavior of a certain class of sequential circuits. Figure 3.10(a) shows an FSM having four states. One approach to modeling FSMs uses two procedures, an approach we now describe.

MULTIPLE ALWAYS PROCEDURES AND SHARED VARIABLES

Because FSMs eventually get implemented as a state register and combinational logic, as shown in Figure 3.10(b), a common approach for describing an FSM uses two always procedures, illustrated in Figure 3.11. One procedure describes a state register for the FSM, and the other procedure describes the combinational function that computes the next state and the outputs based on the current state and inputs. Those two always procedures represent two concurrently-executing components.

The description declares two 2-bit variables, *State* and *StateNext*. The variables are each two bits due to four states requiring at least a 2-bit encoding, where those encodings will be for the values 0, 1, 2, and 3.

The convention of using state names that begin with "*S_*" helps to make clear that those identifiers represent states. The convention also helps avoid conflicts with keywords — for example, *wait* is a reserved word, while *S_wait* is not.

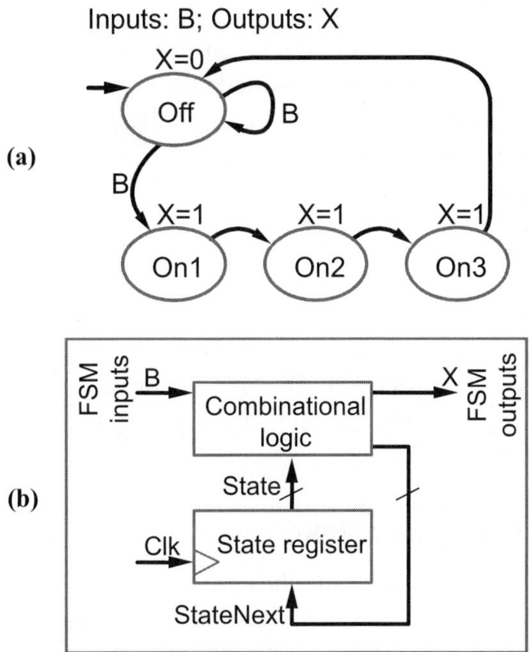

Figure 3.10 FSMs: (a) an FSM state diagram, (b) the sequential circuit implementation model.

```
`timescale 1 ns/1 ns

module LaserTimer(B, X, Clk, Rst);

   input B;
   output reg X;
   input Clk, Rst;

   parameter S_Off = 0, S_On1 = 1,
             S_On2 = 2, S_On3 = 3;

   reg [1:0] State, StateNext;

   // CombLogic
   always @(State, B) begin
      ...
   end

   // StateReg
   always @(posedge Clk) begin
      ...
   end
endmodule
```

Figure 3.11 Two-procedure FSM behavioral description approach.

The two variables are shared by the two always procedures of Figure 3.11. According to Figure 3.10(b), the *CombLogic* procedure should be sensitive to *State* and *B*, and will set values for *StateNext* and *X*. The *StateReg* procedure models a register and is thus sensitive only to the clock input *Clk*. The procedure will set a value for *State*.

PARAMETERS (CONSTANTS)

The description declares four parameter items: *S_Off*, *S_On1*, *S_On2*, and *S_On3*, each one corresponding to a state of the FSM. A ***parameter*** is not a variable or a net, but rather is a constant. A constant is a value that must be initialized when declared, and cannot be changed within the module's definition. The description initializes the four parameters to the decimal numbers 0, 1, 2, and 3, respectively. Declaring parameters for the states of the FSM allows the description to refer to states by name instead of by specific state encodings and improves the readability of the description.

PROCEDURES WITH CASE STATEMENTS

The *CombLogic* procedure can be described using the case statement shown in Figure 3.12. A ***case statement*** selects for execution one statement among several possible statements, based on the value of an expression. In the figure, the expression is simply *State*. The possible values of *State* are the expressions *S_Off*, *S_On1*, *S_On2*, and *S_On3*, where each expression is part of a ***case item*** that includes an associated statement, which is commonly

```
// CombLogic
always @(State, B) begin
   case (State)
      S_Off: begin
         X <= 0;
         if (B == 0)
            StateNext <= S_Off;
         else
            StateNext <= S_On1;
      end
      S_On1: begin
         X <= 1;
         StateNext <= S_On2;
      end
      S_On2: begin
         X <= 1;
         StateNext <= S_On3;
      end
      S_On3: begin
         X <= 1;
         StateNext <= S_Off;
      end
   endcase
end
```

Figure 3.12 FSM's *CombLogic* procedure.

a sequential (begin-end) block as in this example. The first case item whose expression matches the case statement's expression value will execute, causing remaining case items to be ignored. If no case item expression matches, then nothing executes. The last case item may be listed as "*default: statement*". The ***default*** case item's statement executes if none of the earlier case item expressions matched.

For example, if the case statement executes with *State* being *S_On1*, then the sequential block that would execute is: "*X <= 1; StateNext <= S_On2;*". Describing an FSM involves associating with each case item two things: the actions of the corresponding state, followed by statements describing the transitions from a state. For example, state *S_Off*'s action is "*X <= 0;*". *S_Off*'s next state is computed using an *if-else* statement such that if *B* is *0*, the next state is set to *S_off*, whereas if *B* is *1*, the next state is *S_On1*, corresponding to the transitions leaving *S_Off* in the FSM diagram in Figure 3.10(a).

The *StateReg* procedure is shown in Figure 3.13. The procedure is similar to the register procedure introduced in Section 3.1. The procedure is sensitive to a positive clock edge. The procedure checks if the reset input is *1*, in which case the procedure sets the current state variable to the FSM's initial state, meaning *S_Off*. If the reset input is not *1*, then the procedure simply stores its data input, *StateNext*, into *State*.

Note that the two procedures are similar to a two-module approach, except that the interfaces are not specified using ports, but rather using shared variables.

One could instead describe an FSM using a single procedure. That procedure would have the same form as the procedure in Figure 3.13, with the *else*'s single statement

```
...
   parameter S_Off = 0, S_On1 = 1,
             S_On2 = 2, S_On3 = 3;

   reg [1:0] State, StateNext;

...

   // StateReg
   always @(posedge Clk) begin
      if (Rst == 1 )
         State <= S_Off;
      else
         State <= StateNext;
   end
...
```

Figure 3.13 FSM's *StateReg* procedure.

replaced by the complete *case* statement of Figure 3.12. However, a two-procedure approach has two advantages. First, some automatic circuit creation tools may not create a simple state register and combinational logic implementation from the procedure of the single-procedure approach, instead creating a more complex circuit. Second, the single-procedure approach becomes complicated when describing a Mealy FSM, which is a type of FSM whose outputs may change asynchronously when inputs change. Such asynchronous behavior is easily captured in the two procedure approach, whose combinational logic procedure is already asynchronous. In contrast, the single procedure would need to be extended to be sensitive to both the clock and to inputs, and to have part of the code as synchronous and the other part as asynchronous, resulting in a rather awkward description that may not correspond directly to the register and combinational logic implementation model for an FSM.

[SIMUL] SELF-CHECKING TESTBENCHES

Figure 3.14 shows the key parts of a basic testbench for the earlier FSM example. Like the register testbench from Section 3.1, the FSM's testbench has two procedures, one to generate the clock input, and the other to generate test vectors. The vector procedure first initializes the FSM to the FSM's initial state, by setting *Rst_s* to *1*, and then waiting for a rising clock edge. Following good convention, the procedure also sets the input *B_s* to a specific value, in this case *0*, during initialization. Next (after waiting 5 ns before setting new test vectors), the procedure provides a sequence of values on the FSM's input *B_s* for a number of clock cycles. Notice that the testbench doesn't explicitly set the inputs on every clock cycle, relying instead on the fact that the inputs maintain their previous values. Some would argue that better practice involves setting every input explicitly on every cycle. For modules with only a few inputs, explicitly setting every input may be feasible, but large numbers of inputs may result in such explicit setting yielding too many lines of code.

```
...
   // Clock Procedure
   always begin
      Clk_s <= 0;
      #10;
      Clk_s <= 1;
      #10;
   end    // Note: Procedure repeats

   // Vector Procedure
   initial begin
      Rst_s <= 1;
      B_s <= 0;
      @(posedge Clk_s);
      #5 Rst_s <= 0;
      @(posedge Clk_s);
      #5 B_s <= 1;
      @(posedge Clk_s);
      #5 B_s <= 0;
      @(posedge Clk_s);
      @(posedge Clk_s);
      @(posedge Clk_s);
   end
endmodule
```

Figure 3.14 Basic testbench for an FSM.

The waveforms resulting from simulating the testbench appear in Figure 3.15. We can manually examine these waveforms to determine whether the FSM behaves as expected for the given input vectors. We see that *B_s* becomes *1* for one clock cycle, and we know from Figure 3.10(a) that the FSM should output *X_s=1* for three clock cycles after such an occurrence. We see in the waveform that *X_s* indeed becomes *1* for three cycles after *B_s* became *1*, thus increasing our confidence that the FSM description is correct.

Examining waveforms manually in the above manner is tedious and prone to errors, especially when the testbench generates thousands of test vectors rather than just a few. In a more automated ***self-checking testbench*** approach, shown in Figure 3.16, the testbench itself checks for expected behavior, and prints an error message if unexpected behavior is

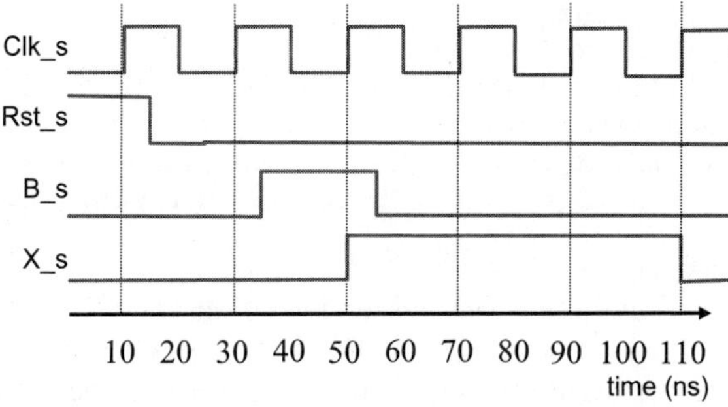

Figure 3.15 Waveform for FSM's testbench.

found. The testbench in Figure 3.16 has its first self-checking if statement just after initializing the FSM. Because the FSM should set output *X_s* to *0* in the initial state *S_Off*, the if statement checks if *X_s* is not *0*. If *X_s* is not *0*, then the if statement's body is executed, causing printing of the error message "*15: Reset failed*".

$display is a built-in Verilog system task for printing information to a display during simulation. ***System tasks*** and ***system functions*** are procedures that interact with the simulator and/or the simulator's host computer system, to carry out behaviors like writing to a display, reading from a file, or obtaining the current simulation time. System tasks and functions begin with a "*$*" to distinguish them from regular tasks and functions. More on system tasks and functions will be presented in Chapter 4. The *$display* task is commonly called with a string argument, such as *$display("Hello")*, which would print the word *Hello*, automatically followed by a newline. The string argument is printed literally, except when special sequences appear in the string. One such sequence is *%t*, which indicates that a time expression should be printed. A time expression must be the next argument within the *$display* task after the string argument. In Figure 3.16, the expression is the value returned by a call to a system function ***$time***, which returns the present simulation time. Thus, the statement "*$display("%t: Reset failed", $time);*" in Figure 3.16 would print "*15: Reset failed*", because the simulation time at that statement is 15 ns.

A self-checking testbench relieves the designer from the tedious task of manually examining lengthy waveforms to determine whether those waveforms match expected behavior. Care should be taken to ensure the self-checking testbench is correct itself.

```
// Vector Procedure
initial begin
   Rst_s <= 1;
   B_s <= 0;
   @(posedge Clk_s);
   #5 if (X_s != 0)
      $display("%t: Reset failed", $time);
   Rst_s <= 0;
   @(posedge Clk_s);
   #5 B_s <= 1;
   @(posedge Clk_s);
   #5 B_s <= 0;
   if (X_s != 1)
      $display("%t: First X=1 failed", $time);
   @(posedge Clk_s);
   #5 if (X_s != 1)
      $display("%t: Second X=1 failed", $time);
   @(posedge Clk_s);
   #5 if (X_s != 1)
      $display("%t: Third X=1 failed", $time);
   @(posedge Clk_s);
   #5 if (X_s != 0)
      $display("%t: Final X=0 failed", $time);
end
```

Figure 3.16 Self-checking testbench for an FSM. (Note: Vertical space between vectors would improve readability, but is omitted here for space reasons.)

3.3 TOP-DOWN DESIGN—FSMS TO CONTROLLER STRUCTURE

As discussed in the previous chapter, a top-down design approach involves first capturing behavior and simulating, and then creating structure and simulating again. The previous section showed how to capture FSM behavior and simulate that behavior. This section proceeds with the top-down approach, to create structure and simulate again.

Figure 3.17 illustrates the steps involved in converting an FSM to a structural controller implementation of that FSM. The first step creates the architecture, consisting of a 2-bit state register, and combinational logic, as in Figure 3.17(a). The next step encodes the states using unique bit representations, as shown in Figure 3.17(b). The encoding results in the state table of Figure 3.17(c). From this state table, one can derive the combinational logic equations of Figure 3.17(d). Implementing those equations as a circuit inside the combinational logic block of Figure 3.17(a) would complete the controller design.

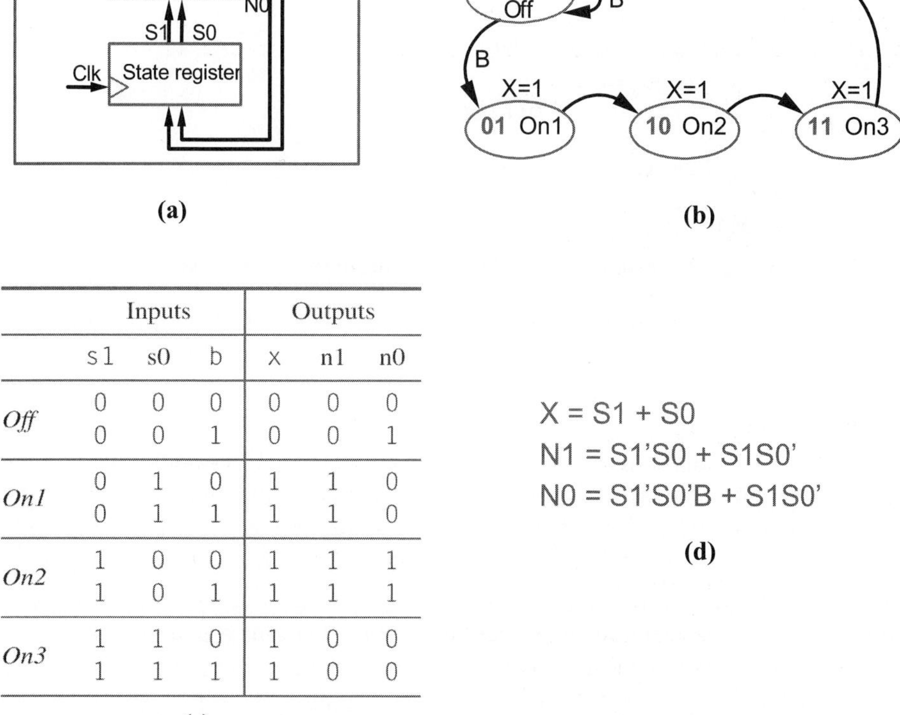

	Inputs			Outputs		
	s1	s0	b	x	n1	n0
Off	0	0	0	0	0	0
	0	0	1	0	0	1
On1	0	1	0	1	1	0
	0	1	1	1	1	0
On2	1	0	0	1	1	1
	1	0	1	1	1	1
On3	1	1	0	1	0	0
	1	1	1	1	0	0

(c)

X = S1 + S0
N1 = S1'S0 + S1S0'
N0 = S1'S0'B + S1S0'

(d)

Figure 3.17 Top-down FSM to controller design: (a) architecture, (b) encoded states, (c) state table, (d) combinational logic.

```
`timescale 1 ns/1 ns

module LaserTimer(B, X, Clk, Rst);

   input B;
   output reg X;
   input Clk, Rst;

   parameter S_Off = 2'b00;

   reg [1:0] State, StateNext;
   // State encodings:
   //    S_Off 00, S_On1 01, S_On2 10, S_On3 11

   // CombLogic
   always @(State, B) begin
      X <= State[1] | State[0];
      StateNext[1] <= (~State[1] & State[0])
                    | (State[1] & ~State[0]);
      StateNext[0] <= (~State[1] & ~State[0] & B)
                    | (State[1] & ~State[0]);
   end

   // StateReg
   always @(posedge Clk) begin
      if (Rst == 1 )
         State <= S_Off;
      else
         State <= StateNext;
   end
endmodule
```

Figure 3.18 Controller description for earlier-introduced FSM.

Figure 3.18 shows the controller description of the FSM. This description differs from the original FSM description shown in Figure 3.11, Figure 3.12, and Figure 3.13, in several ways.

First, only the encoding "*00*" for the initial state *S_Off* is declared as a parameter. That parameter is used to initialize the state register during a reset. The remaining state encodings are never explicitly used and thus are not declared, instead being listed in a comment.

Second, the combinational logic procedure now directly models the combinational functions using equations, rather than indirectly modeling those functions using a case statement. Note how much less the equations convey the intended system behavior to the reader, compared to the case statement, even though the equations are more compact.

The controller description has exactly the same input and output ports as did the earlier FSM description. The controller description can be simulated using the same testbench as in Section 3.2, resulting in the same waveforms as in Figure 3.15.

Although we said the controller description represented "structure," notice that the combinational logic procedure is actually a behavioral description of the combinational logic, rather than a structural description. Such behavioral description of combinational logic was covered in Chapter 2. That combinational behavior could be further refined, again using top-down design approach, to create a structural connection of gates for the combinational logic. Note that the top-down design process may be repeated for different parts of a design, until finally reaching a structural circuit consisting of low-level components.

[SYNTH] COMMON PITFALL

Not assigning outputs in every state

A common mistake when describing FSMs is to not assign every FSM output in every state. Failing to assign an output means the output's value will be remembered, rather than updated, by the procedure during a particular clock cycle. That remembered value means the output has storage, and thus that the output is not just determined by the present state as is intended. Simulation may not unveil the storage if test vectors are not thorough enough, but synthesis tools will either refuse to synthesize such a circuit, report a warning during synthesis, or generate a circuit that behaves different from a designer's expectations.

Many experienced designers avoid this problem using one of two methods. One method is to ensure every output is assigned in every state, perhaps by cut-and-pasting a sequence of assignment statements, which includes every output, into every case item, with each sequence requiring completion with a specific assigned values.

Another method is to initially assign every output to a default value before the case statement, as illustrated in Figure 3.19. If an output does not get assigned by a case item during execution of the case statement, the initially assigned value will be the actual assigned value for that output during that execution of the procedure. However, if that output does get assigned in a case item, then that assignment overrides the initial assignment. In Figure 3.19, the FSM's output *X* is initialized to *0*. If procedure execution executes any of the *S_On* case items, the assignment of *X* to *1* will override the earlier assignment to *0*. If procedure execution instead executes the *S_Off* alternative, *X* will be set to *0*.

Notice that the assignment to *0* in *S_Off*'s statements is redundant with the assignment to *0* during initialization, and could be eliminated. However, it may be best to leave that assignment there to make the behavior of state *S_Off* entirely clear.

The initialization method of avoiding the pitfall is useful when an FSM has many outputs, because the method improves the readability of each case item. Only the outputs that are assigned a different value from the default value, or for which a designer wishes to clearly show being assigned a value in a state, need be included in each case item. Figure 3.20 illustrates such improved readability. Figure 3.20(a) shows all outputs assigned in every state. Figure 3.20(b) shows only the relevant output assignments for each—clearly, state *S* assigns *B* to *1*, and state *T* assigns *C* to *1*. Note that such output initialization can be used to support the common simplifying FSM notation that assumes every output not explicitly assigned in a state is implicitly assigned *0*, as illustrated in the Figure 3.20(b).

```
// CombLogic
always @(State, B) begin
   X <= 0;
   case (State)
      S_Off: begin
         X <= 0;
         if (B == 0)
            StateNext <= S_Off;
         else
            StateNext <= S_On1;
      end
      S_On1: begin
         X <= 1;
         StateNext <= S_On2;
      end
      S_On2: begin
         X <= 1;
         StateNext <= S_On3;
      end
      S_On3: begin
         X <= 1;
         StateNext <= S_Off;
      end
   endcase
end
```

Could delete this without changing behavior (but probably clearer to keep it)

Figure 3.19 Initializing FSM outputs.

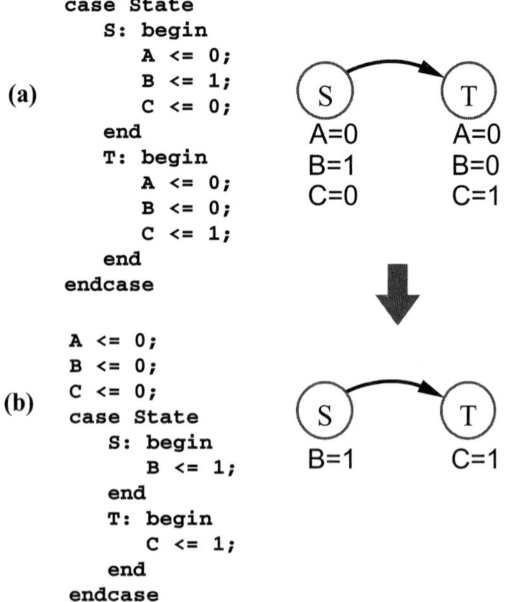
(a)
case State
S: begin
A <= 0;
B <= 1;
C <= 0;
end
T: begin
A <= 0;
B <= 0;
C <= 1;
end
endcase
S
T
A=0
B=1
C=0
A=0
B=0
C=1
(b)
A <= 0;
B <= 0;
C <= 0;
case State
S: begin
B <= 1;
end
T: begin
C <= 1;
end
endcase
S
T
B=1
C=1

Figure 3.20 FSM: (a) without initialization, (b) with initialization, which improves readability.

3.4 MORE SIMULATION CONCEPTS

[SIMUL] THE SIMULATION CYCLE

It can be instructive to learn how a simulator executes an HDL description to generate waveforms. This section will highlight how a simulator might execute the example description in Figure 3.21. HDL simulation is complex; this section provides a greatly simplified description just to convey the basic idea.

The example has three user-defined register variables: *Q*, *Clk*, and *S*. The job of the simulator is to determine values for all variables and nets over time. The simulator will accomplish this job by repeatedly executing and suspending the three procedures *P1*, *P2*, and *P3*, while keeping track of the simulated time, known as ***simulation time***.

At the start of simulation, all bits have the unknown value *x*, as shown in Figure 3.22(b) under the heading *Start*, and the simulation time is 0 ns. The simulator then executes each

```
`timescale 1 ns/1 ns

module SimEx1(Q);

   output reg Q;
   reg Clk, S;

   // P1
   always begin
      Clk <= 0;
      #10;
      Clk <= 1;
      #10;
   end

   // P2
   always @(S) begin
      Q <= ~S;
   end

   // P3
   initial begin
      @ (posedge Clk);
      S <= 1;
      @ (posedge Clk);
      S <= 0;
   end

endmodule
```

Figure 3.21 Example to demonstrate simulation concepts.

(a)

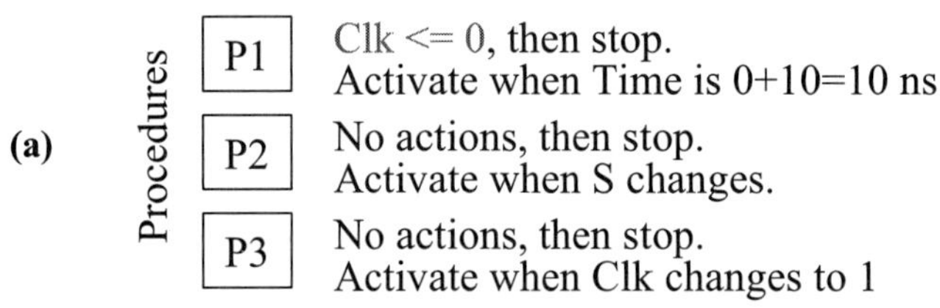

(b)

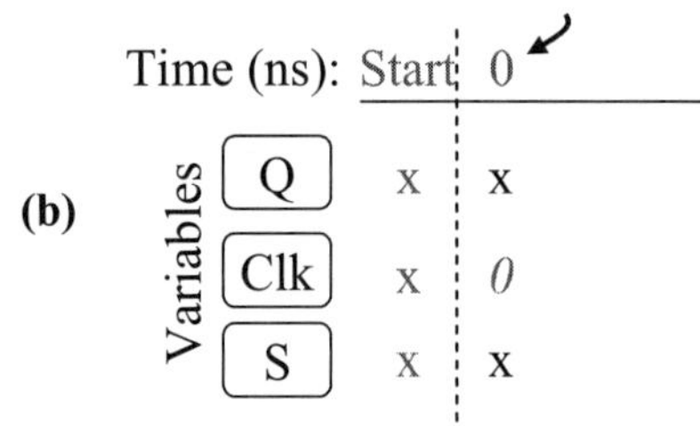

Figure 3.22 Simulation initialization: (a) Procedure execution and stopping, (b) variable values.

procedure, one at a time in any order, until each procedure stops due to a delay control or event control. As shown in Figure 3.22(a), the simulator will execute procedure *P1*'s first statement "*Clk* <= *0;*" and then stop at the delay control "*#10;*". The simulator will note that *P1* should resume execution 10 ns after the present simulation time of 0 ns, meaning *P1* should activate at time 0 ns + 10 ns = 10 ns. The simulator will then execute procedure *P2*, which stops at the event control. The simulator will note that this procedure should activate when *S* changes. Finally, the simulator will execute *P3* and stop at the event control "*@(posedge Clk);*". The simulator will note that this procedure should activate when *Clk* changes to *1*. The variable values will be those shown for time 0 ns in Figure 3.22(b).

The simulator will continue simulation by repeatedly executing the simulation cycle. During each ***simulation cycle***, the simulator advances simulation time to the next time at which a procedure (or procedures) activates, and executes the active procedure(s) until the procedure(s) stops again. If more than one procedure is active, the simulator can execute them in any order. In this case, the simulator will advance time to 10 ns, at which time procedure *P1* activates, as shown in Figure 3.23(a). The simulator executes *P1,* thus executing the statement "*Clk* <= *1;*", and then stopping at the delay control "*#10;*". As before, the simulator notes that this procedure should activate 10 ns after the present simulation time of 10 ns, meaning *P1* should activate again at time 20 ns.

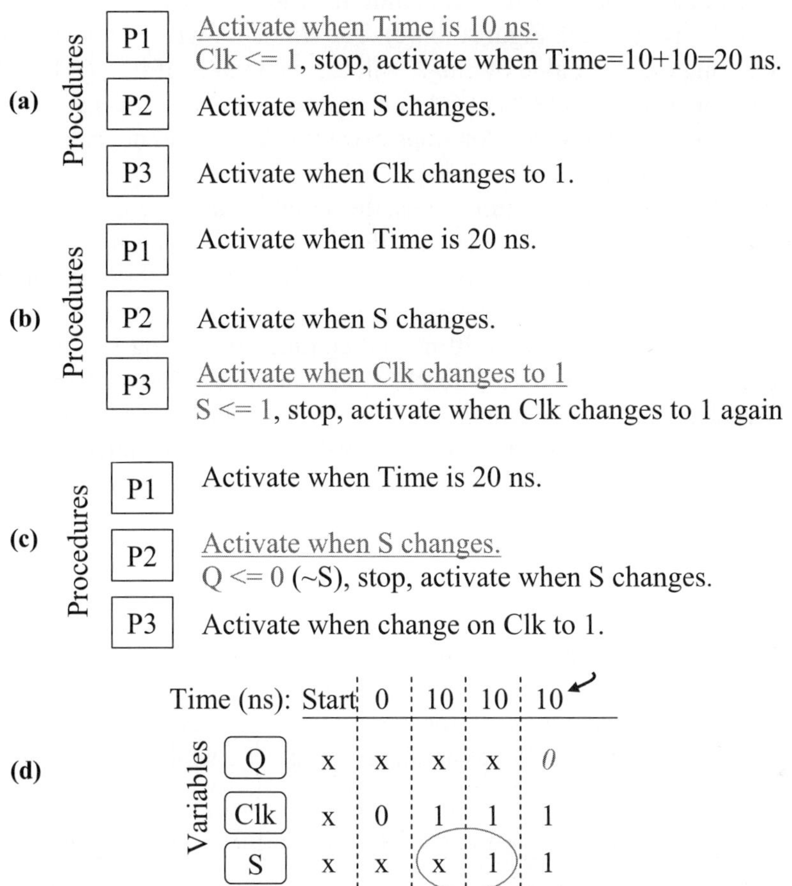

Figure 3.23 Simulation execution: (a)-(c) Procedure execution and suspension, (d) variable values during simulation execution, highlighting activation and update from (c).

The simulator then advances simulation time to the next time at which a procedure activates. Remember that the simulator previously noted that *P3* should activate when *Clk* changes to *1*. During execution of *P1*, the simulator updated the value of *Clk* to *1* and should thus now activate *P3*. Thus, to execute *P3*, the simulator "advances" time to 10 ns. In this case, the simulator "advances" the simulation time to the current time (i.e., "advancing" from 10 ns to 10 ns), indicating that additional procedures need to be executed at this current time. After advancing the simulation time, the simulator executes *P3* by executing the statement "*S <= 1;*" and then stops at the following statement "*@ (posedge Clk);*". The simulator notes that this procedure should activate again when *Clk* changes to *1*, as shown in Figure 3.23(b).

Procedure *P2* was previously stopped at the event control "*@(S)*". While executing *P3*, the simulator updated the value of S from *x* to *1* and thus now needs to execute *P2*. To do so, the simulator will again advance the simulation time to the current time of 10 ns. The simulator executes *P2*, as shown in Figure 3.23(c). The simulator will execute the statement "*Q <= ~S;*" and seeing that the value of *S* is *1*, will assign a value of *0* to *Q*. Reaching the end of *P2*, which is an always procedure and thus repeats, the simulator reaches the event control "*@(S)*" again, where the simulator stops execution of *P2* and notes that *P2* should activate when *S* changes again.

After several simulation cycles at time 10 ns, the variable values will be the last values shown for time 10 ns in Figure 3.23(d). Note that during simulation, the simulator will keep track of the variable values as the simulator executes each procedure, but the output waveforms will only show the final variable values at the end of the current time.

The simulator will advance time to 20 ns and continue executing simulation cycles, until the user-specified simulation time is reached. The variable values determined during simulation will translate to an output simulation waveform, as shown in Figure 3.24. Notice how the waveform values correspond to the final values of each simulation time determined during simulation.

[SIMUL] SCHEDULED EVENTS

In describing the simulation cycle of a simulator, we assumed that updates to a variable's value happened immediately. In fact, assignments using "<=" do not update the variable's value immediately. An assignment in a procedure using "<=" is called a non-blocking assignment statement, in contrast to an assignment using "=", which is called a blocking

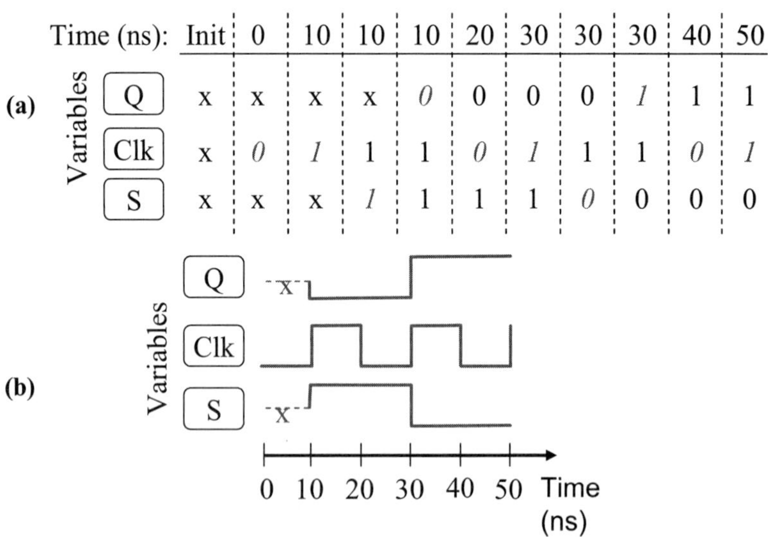

Figure 3.24 Simulation results: (a) Variable values over time as computed during simulation, (b) waveforms derived from those values.

assignment statement and will be described in a later chapter. Instead, the assignment ***schedules*** a change by placing an assign update ***event*** on an event queue. The queue will be processed, and hence the variable's value will be updated, at the end of the simulation cycle. We need to revise the previous explanation of a simulation cycle to include updating variable values using the queue. In the revised explanation of a simulation cycle, the simulator advances simulation time to the next time at which a procedure (or procedures) will resume, executes the resumed procedure(s) until the procedure(s) stops, *and then updates variables with scheduled assign update events*.

It is important to consider the implications of this revised explanation of a simulation cycle. One implication is that the execution order of procedures during a simulation cycle (usually[3]) does not matter. For example, consider the two procedures, *Proc1* and *Proc2*, shown in Figure 3.25. Assume that both procedures are activated during the same simulation cycle, and assume that *B* is *0*. The simulator may execute *Proc1*, thus executing the statement "*B <= ~B;*", scheduling an assign update event of *B* to *1*, and stopping execution of the procedure. Within the same simulation cycle, the simulator will execute *Proc2*, execute the statement "*A <= B;*", and schedule an assign update event of *A* to *0*. Note that during execution of those procedures, the current value of *B* stays *0*. At the end of the simulation cycle, the scheduled events will be processed, causing *B* to be updated to *1*, and *A* to be updated to *0*. The order in which the simulator executes the two procedures does not matter.

Another implication is that the execution order of non-blocking assignments to different variables within a procedure does not matter. Consider the two alternative procedures,

Assume B is 0.

Proc1:

```
B <= ~B;
```

Proc2:

```
A <= B;
```

A will be 0, not 1.

Figure 3.25 Scheduled assign update events: Variable values are updated at the end of the simulation cycle.

[3]The Verilog standard gives simulators some flexibility in executing multiple active procedures, which in some circumstances can lead to non-deterministic simulation results. However, the straightforward coding style used in this book should not lead to such circumstances.

Proc3a: ←	Same →	Proc3b:
`C <= ~C;`		`D <= C;`
`D <= C;`		`C <= ~C;`

Figure 3.26 Scheduled assign update events: Order of assignments to different variables within a procedure does not matter.

Proc3a and *Proc3b*, shown in Figure 3.26. These two procedures consist of the same two assignment statements, "*C <= ~C;*" and "*D <= C;*", but with opposite statement ordering. Assume the current value of *C* is *0*. Regardless of which procedure we write, after executing the procedure, *C* will be *1* and *D* will be *0*. Each assignment statement uses the current value, not the scheduled value, of *C* to determine the next values for *C* and *D*. The assignment statements do not modify the present value of *C* or *D*, but rather schedule updates. Thus, both procedures have the same behavior even though the assignments to *C* and *D* have different orders within the two procedures. For example, when executing *Proc3a*, the simulator will execute the statement "*C <= ~C;*" and schedule an assign update of *C* to *1* (because C is presently 0). When executing the following statement, "*D <= C;*", the simulator will use the current value of *C* (which is *0*), not the scheduled value of *1*, and will thus schedule an assign update of *D* to *0*.

Scheduled assign update events further imply that later assignments to a particular variable within a procedure have precedence over earlier assignments to that same variable. Consider the procedure example in Figure 3.27. The simulator will execute the statement "*E <= 0;*" and thus schedule an assign update event of *E* to *0*. However, the simulator then executes the statement "*E <= 1;*" further down in the procedure, and thus the simulator will schedule an assign update event of *E* to *1*. When processing the event queue at the end of the simulation cycle, the simulator will process the event setting *E* to *0*, but then soon after process the event assigning *E* to *1*. Thus, at the end of the simulation cycle, *E* will be *1*, meaning the earlier assignment to *0* is effectively overwritten. Further recall the FSM example in Figure 3.19. That FSM's implementation took advantage of the fact that later output assignments (the assignment within a state's case item) have precedence over earlier assignments (the default output assignment before the case statement).

Proc4:

```
E <= 0;
...
E <= 1;
```

Figure 3.27 Scheduled assign update events: Later non-blocking assignments overwrite earlier assignments.

3.5 RESETS

Reset behavior is the behavior of a register (or other sequential element, like a flip-flop) that occurs when a special reset input is asserted. For example, the register described in Figure 3.2 included reset behavior that cleared the register to *0*s when an input *Rst* equaled *1*, and the register described in Figure 3.13 had reset behavior that initialized the register to the value "*S_Off*" when an input *Rst* equaled *1*. Good design practice dictates having a defined reset behavior for every register in a design, thus ensuring that a design always starts from the same starting point. Reset behavior should always have priority over normal register operation.

Reset behavior usually clears a register to *0*s, but may instead initialize a register to a specific non-zero value, such as when initializing a controller's state register to the encoding of the initial state of an FSM. A system's reset input is typically asserted externally at the start of operation of a sequential circuit, such as when a chip is first powered on. However, resets can also occur during circuit operation, perhaps due to a detected failure, due to a user request, or for some other reason.

The previous examples of Figure 3.2 and Figure 3.13 used a reset technique known as synchronous reset. A ***synchronous reset*** is a reset that, when asserted, only takes effect at the next rising clock. Figure 3.28(b) shows the behavior of the synchronous reset of the register described in Figure 3.2, whose description is shown again in Figure 3.28(a) for convenience. The setting of *Rst* to *1* has no effect until a rising clock edge arrives, at which time the reset of the register to *0*s takes place.

A second reset technique is known as asynchronous reset. An ***asynchronous reset*** is a reset that takes effect almost immediately after being asserted, independently from the clock input. Figure 3.28(c) provides a description of the same register from Figure 3.28(a) except that the register's reset behavior is now described to be asynchronous. To achieve an asynchronous reset, the description includes "*posedge Rst*" in the sensitivity list of the always procedure—if *Rst* were omitted, the procedure would only check the *Rst* input when the clock input changed, and thus the reset would be synchronous. For the reset behavior to have priority over normal operation, the check for *Rst* equal to *1* must occur before the check for a rising clock, and the check for a rising clock must be an *else* part rather than a separate *if* statement. Figure 3.28(d) illustrates the behavior of this asynchronous reset. The setting of *Rst* to *1* has an effect almost immediately (when *Rst* changes from its initial value of *x* to *1*, which is also a positive edge), causing the reset of the register to *0*s.

```
`timescale 1 ns/1 ns

module Reg4(I, Q, Clk, Rst);

   input [3:0] I;
   output [3:0] Q;
   reg [3:0] Q;
   input Clk, Rst;

   always @(posedge Clk) begin
      if (Rst == 1 )
         Q <= 4'b0000;
      else
         Q <= I;
   end
endmodule
```

(a)

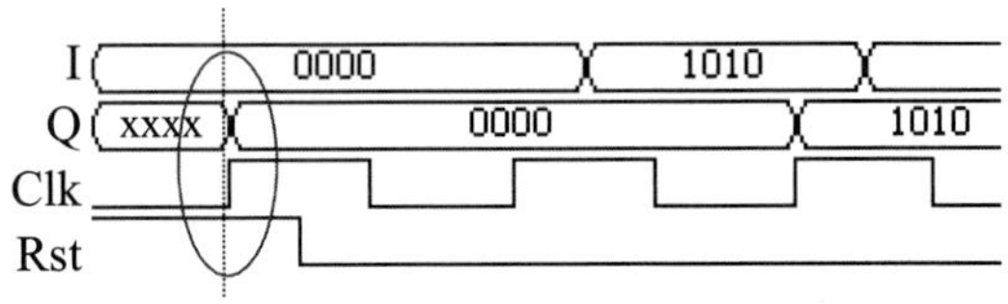

I 0000 1010
Q xxxx 0000 1010
Clk
Rst

(b)

```
`timescale 1 ns/1 ns

module Reg4(I, Q, Clk, Rst);

   input [3:0] I;
   output [3:0] Q;
   reg [3:0] Q;
   input Clk, Rst;

   always @(posedge Clk, posedge Rst) begin
      if (Rst == 1 )
         Q <= 4'b0000;
      else
         Q <= I;
   end
endmodule
```

(c)

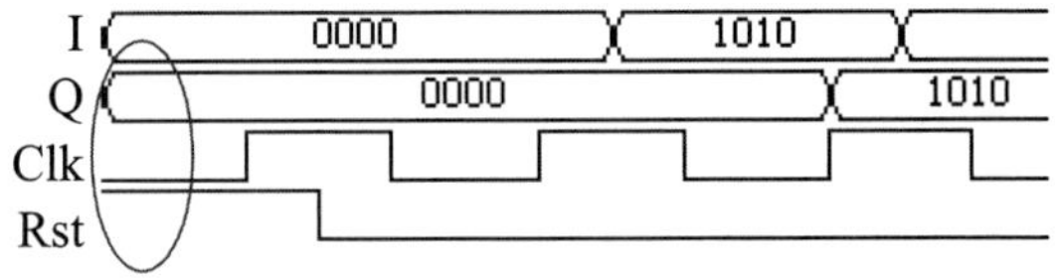

I 0000 1010
Q 0000 1010
Clk
Rst

(d)

Figure 3.28 Reset techniques: (a) synchronous reset, (b) synchronous reset has no effect until next rising clock, (c) asynchronous reset, (d) asynchronous reset has effect almost immediately, independently from the clock.

(a)

```
...
   // StateReg
   always @(posedge Clk) begin
      if (Rst == 1 )
         State <= S_Off;
      else
         State <= StateNext;
   end
...
```

(b)

```
...
   // StateReg
   always @(posedge Clk, posedge Rst) begin
      if (Rst == 1 )
         State <= S_Off;
      else
         State <= StateNext;
   end
...
```

Figure 3.29 FSM's *StateReg* procedure with: (a) synchronous reset, (b) asynchronous reset.

The state register procedure from Figure 3.13, shown again in Figure 3.29(a) for convenience, could have also been described to use an asynchronous reset rather than a synchronous reset, as shown in Figure 3.29(b).

Whether designers should use synchronous or asynchronous resets is a hotly debated subject in the design community. Each approach has pros and cons. For example, asynchronous resets can reset a circuit even if the clock is not functioning. On the other hand, synchronous resets may make timing analysis a bit easier. The debate cannot be settled here. The important thing is to be consistent in the use of resets throughout a design. All registers should have defined reset behavior that takes priority over normal register behavior, and that reset behavior should all be synchronous reset or should all be asynchronous reset. This book will use synchronous resets in the remaining examples.

3.6 DESCRIBING SAFE FSMS

A ***safe FSM*** is an FSM whose definition is such that if the FSM were to ever enter an illegal state, the FSM would transition to a legal state. Figure 3.30(a) shows an unsafe FSM. The FSM uses a 2-bit state encoding but has only three states, resulting in one illegal state encoded as "*11*". Such an illegal state is also called an *unreachable* state. In theory, an illegal state can never be reached during operation of the FSM. In practice, however, such a state may be reached due to a circuit error. For example, severe electrical noise could result in a bit change from *0* to *1* or vice versa. If an illegal state is reached, the FSM's behavior is undefined. A circuit synthesized for that FSM could conceivably get stuck in such an illegal state (or begin transitioning among illegal states).

Figure 3.30(b) shows a safe version of the same FSM, in which the illegal state is explicitly included in the FSM. That state transitions to state *Off*, while outputting *X=0*. Although the state looks odd due to having no transitions leading to the state, remember that the state can only be reached due to a circuit error.

Figure 3.31(a) shows a description of an unsafe FSM. Only the legal states appear in the description. Synthesis of a controller from this FSM might result in the creation of an unsafe controller. Some synthesis tools support a "safe" synthesis option that automatically converts an unsafe FSM description into a safe FSM during synthesis.

In contrast, Figure 3.31(b) explicitly describes a safe FSM. The description makes use of a *default* case item in a case statement. A case statement may contain one default case item, which must be the last case item of the case statement, and which is chosen only if none of the earlier items match.

Note that the default case item approach enables safe FSM description even before the FSM states have been encoded.

Good practice dictates including a default case item in all state machines. One might believe that the default case item is not needed if the number of states is a power of two. However, before states have been encoded, there is no guarantee that a synthesis tool will

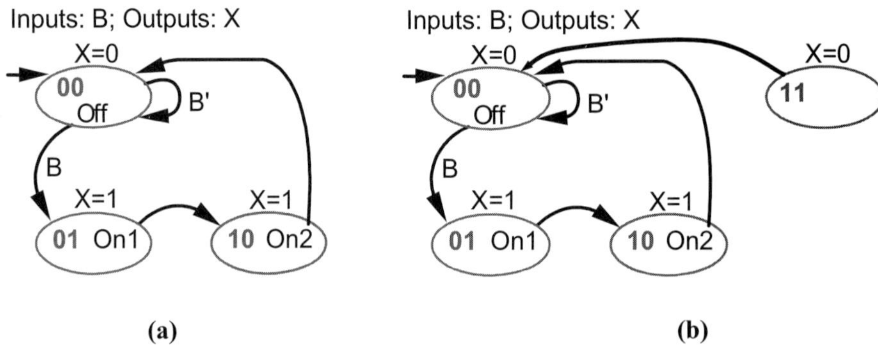

Figure 3.30 Unsafe versus safe FSMs: (a) unsafe FSM may get stuck in an undefined state ("*11*"), (b) safe FSM explicitly transitions from undefined states back to a defined state.

```
...
   reg [1:0] State, StateNext;

   always @(State, B) begin
     case (State)
        S_Off: begin
           X <= 0;
           if (B == 0)
              StateNext <= S_Off;
           else
              StateNext <= S_On1;
        end
        S_On1: begin
           X <= 1;
           StateNext <= S_On2;
        end
        S_On2: begin
           X <= 1;
           StateNext <= S_Off;
        end
     endcase
   end
...
```

(a)

```
...
   reg [1:0] State, StateNext;

   always @(State, B) begin
     case (State)
        S_Off: begin
           X <= 0;
           if (B == 0)
              StateNext <= S_Off;
           else
              StateNext <= S_On1;
        end
        S_On1: begin
           X <= 1;
           StateNext <= S_On2;
        end
        S_On2: begin
           X <= 1;
           StateNext <= S_Off;
        end
        default: begin
           X <= 0;
           StateNext <= S_Off;
        end
     endcase
   end
...
```

(b)

Figure 3.31 Unsafe versus safe FSM descriptions: (a) unsafe FSM description only lists legal states, (b) safe FSM description uses default case item to cover illegal states, which all transition back to *S_Off*.

encode states using the minimum number of bits. The tool might, for example, encode states using a one-hot encoding, which uses as many bits as there are states in the FSM. Such an encoding will have numerous illegal states. Using a default case item helps ensure that an illegal state will have a defined transition back to a legal state. Thus, including a default case item is typically wise for all state machines.

However, designers should be aware that a synthesis tool could potentially optimize away unreachable states in order to improvement performance and size of a circuit. Thus, if a tool has a "safe" option, it should be selected, even if the state machine's description appears to be safe.

CHAPTER 4

Datapath Components

Dozens of different datapath components exist; the components covered in this chapter form a representative sample, such that the description approach may be applied to other components.

4.1 MULTIFUNCTION REGISTERS

The previous chapter showed a register that had only a reset control input. A more general register may have more control inputs, such as load, shift right, and shift left control inputs, along with data inputs when shifting right or left. Such a multifunction register appears in Figure 4.1(a), with the register's operations appearing in Figure 4.1(b).

Describing a multifunction register could be done structurally, by connecting four flip-flops, four muxes, and combinational logic to convert the control inputs into mux select inputs.

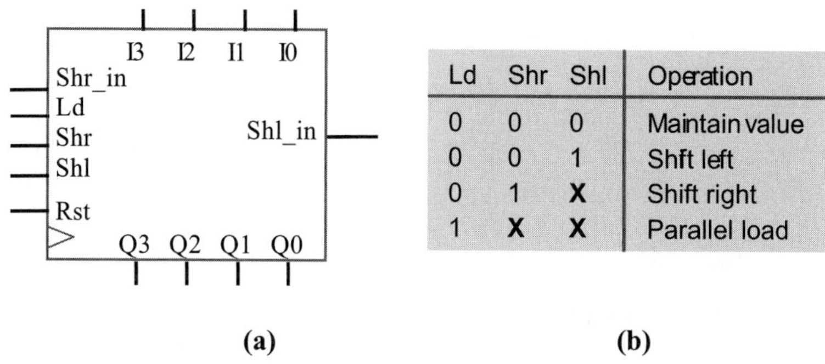

Ld	Shr	Shl	Operation
0	0	0	Maintain value
0	0	1	Shft left
0	1	X	Shift right
1	X	X	Parallel load

Figure 4.1 A multifunction register: (a) block diagram, (b) operation table.

```
`timescale 1 ns/1 ns

module MfReg4(I, Q, Ld, Shr, Shl, Shr_in, Shl_in, Clk, Rst);

    input [3:0] I;
    output [3:0] Q;
    input Ld, Shr, Shl, Shr_in, Shl_in;
    input Clk, Rst;

    reg [3:0] R;

    always @(posedge Clk) begin
       if (Rst == 1)
          R <= 4'b0000;
       else if (Ld == 1)
          R <= I;
       else if (Shr == 1) begin
          R[3] <= Shr_in; R[2] <= R[3];
          R[1] <= R[2]; R[0] <= R[1];
       end
       else if (Shl == 1) begin
          R[0] <= Shl_in; R[1] <= R[0];
          R[2] <= R[1]; R[3] <= R[2];
       end
    end

    assign Q = R;
endmodule
```

Figure 4.2 Multifunction register behavioral description.

The register can instead be described behaviorally, as shown in Figure 4.2. The *if* statement maintains the priorities among the control inputs of Figure 4.1(b), through the ordering of the *else-if* parts. *Rst* has highest priority, then *Ld*, then *Shr*, and finally *Shl*.

When *Shr* is *1*, the shift is accomplished using four statements that assign each bit to the location on the right. Recall that each assignment statement schedules an update rather than making an immediate update, and thus the order of those assignment statements in the description does not matter.

CONTINUOUS ASSIGNMENT STATEMENT

In the register description of Section 3.1, the output port Q, being declared as a reg variable, was used for the register's storage. However, the description in Figure 4.2 uses a register R for storage. The reason for using a distinct variable is that the shift operations require that the description *read* the stored value, but good practice dictates that we never read a module's output port, such as output port *Q* in Figure 4.2, from within the module.

Because the register should output the stored value on port *Q*, a mechanism is needed to copy *R*'s value to port *Q* at all times. The description in Figure 4.2 therefore includes the statement "*assign Q = R;*" near the bottom of the description. However, note that the statement *is not contained within the always procedure*. A ***continuous assignment statement***, having the general form "*assign Net_Name = Expression;*", assigns the given net with the expression's value whenever the value changes. The value on the left side must be a net, not a variable. *Q* will change whenever *R* changes; in a sense, *Q* has been "wired" to *R*. Note that the continuous assignment statement describes combinational logic, where in this case the logic is simply a wire.

Figure 4.3 shows a partial testbench for Figure 4.2's multifunction register. That testbench is actually very short; a good testbench would test all the control inputs, and would test different combinations of those inputs too. Note that the testbench initializes all the component inputs and resets the register. The testbench then loads "*1111*", and then shifts right.

The waveforms resulting from simulating the multifunction register with the given testbench are shown in Figure 4.4. The waveforms show the register being cleared to "*0000*", then loaded with "*1111*", and then shifted right on each of the next four clock cycles, resulting in register values of "*0111*", "*0011*", "*0001*", and finally "*0000*".

One might incorrectly assume that another way to update *Q* with the value of *R* would be to instead add the statement "*Q <= R;*" as the last statement in the

```
...
   // Clock Procedure
   ...

   // Vector Procedure
   initial begin
      Rst_s <= 1;
      I_s <= 4'b0000;
      Ld_s <= 0; Shr_s <= 0; Shl_s <= 0;
      Shr_in_s <= 0; Shl_in_s <= 0;
      @(posedge Clk_s);
      #5 Rst_s <= 0;
      I_s <= 4'b1111; Ld_s <= 1;
      @(posedge Clk_s);
      #5 Ld_s <= 0; Shr_s <= 1;
      // Good testbench needs more vectors
   end
endmodule
```

Figure 4.3. Multifunction register testbench.

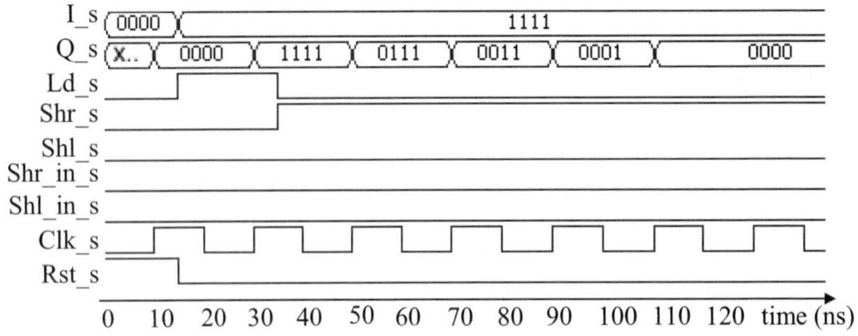

Figure 4.4 Multifunction register waveforms.

always procedure of Figure 4.2, after having declared *Q* to be a reg variable. However, that approach would not correctly describe the desired behavior. Recall that reg variables assigned using "<=" in a procedure do not actually get updated until the end of the simulation cycle. Thus, that last statement added to the procedure would assign *Q* with the *old* value of reg variable *R*, and not with the newly-scheduled value of *R*. *Q* would thus not be updated until the next time the procedure executes, which would be on the next rising clock edge, and thus *Q*'s value would always be one cycle behind what the value should be. In contrast, the continuous assignment "*assign Q = R;*" is not sensitive to the clock input, and instead executes whenever *R* changes (thus executing just one simulation cycle after *R* is updated).

COMMON PITFALL

Not using a begin-end block with every if statement

A common pitfall occurs when designers, seeking more compact code, omit use of a begin-end block when an if statement has only one sub-statement, as in Figure 4.5(a). While the statement works fine initially, problems may occur if another sub-statement is added later, but without also enclosing the sub-statements in begin-end. As shown in the figure, the designer may believe the added display statement is part of the *if* statement, when in fact the statement comes after the *if* statement, and thus executes unconditionally.

The problem can be especially difficult to detect with nested if statements. Consider the "*if (Rst == 1)*" statement in Figure 4.2, which does not follow the begin-end usage guideline. Imagine following the statement "*R <= 4'b0000;*" by the statement "*if (I == 0) $display("Rst with I==0."*"). The "*else if (Ld == 1)*" statement would then become the *else* part of that latter *if* statement ("*if (I == 0)*"), and no longer part of the former *if* statement ("*if (Rst == 1)*"). Such errors can be very hard to find.

To avoid this pitfall, use begin-end with an *if* statement even when the *if* statement only has one sub-statement, as shown in Figure 4.5(b). The same guideline

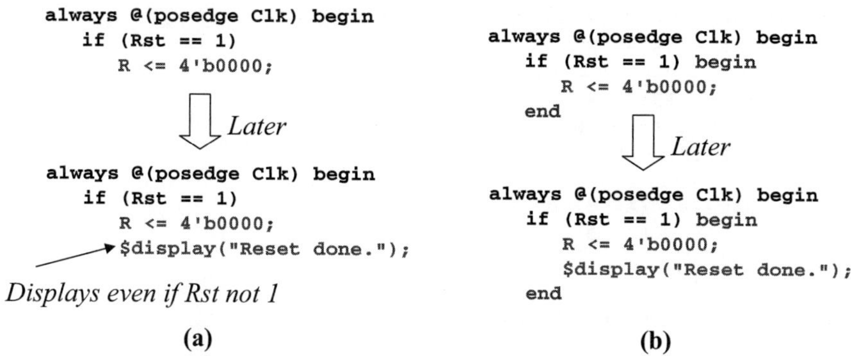
always @(posedge Clk) begin
if (Rst == 1)
R <= 4'b0000;
Later
always @(posedge Clk) begin
if (Rst == 1)
R <= 4'b0000;
$display("Reset done.");
Displays even if Rst not 1
(a)
always @(posedge Clk) begin
if (Rst == 1) begin
R <= 4'b0000;
end
Later
always @(posedge Clk) begin
if (Rst == 1) begin
R <= 4'b0000;
$display("Reset done.");
end
(b)

Figure 4.5 Common pitfall: (a) Not using a begin-end block for an if statement may later yield unexpected behavior when a sub-statement is added, (b) always using begin-end with if statements helps prevent problems later.

applies to an *else* part with only one sub-statement, which should also use a begin-end block.

The reader might examine the earlier description in Figure 4.2 to find situations where a begin-end block should have been inserted to avoid possible future problems.

4.2 ADDERS

An N-bit adder adds two N-bit binary numbers, resulting in an N-bit binary number representing the sum, and resulting in a carry-out bit. The adder may also include a carry-in bit.

One way to describe an N-bit adder is structurally, as a connection of N full-adders, where each full-adder itself is described either as a connection of gates or perhaps as combinational behavior. Of course, such a structural description represents a carry-ripple implementation of an N-bit adder. Other types of adder implementations, such as a carry-lookahead adder, would require a different structural description.

Another way to describe an N-bit adder is behaviorally. A behavioral description could be created to reflect a carry-ripple implementation or a carry-lookahead implementation, but a nice feature of a behavioral description is its ability to indicate just the functionality of a module (in this case, the adding of two numbers), without implying a particular implementation (such as carry-ripple or carry-lookahead).

BUILT-IN ARITHMETIC OPERATIONS

Given two N-bit inputs A and B, the idea of an implementation-neutral behavioral adder description is to simply describe the adder as computing the sum $A + B$. Fig-

```
`timescale 1 ns/1 ns

module Add4(A, B, S);

   input [3:0] A, B;
   output [3:0] S;
   reg [3:0] S;

   always @(A, B) begin
      S <= A + B;
   end
endmodule
```

Figure 4.6 Simple 4-bit adder description.

ure 4.6 shows such a description. The adder has two 4-bit input ports *A* and *B*, and a 4-bit output port *S*. The module consists of a single always procedure, which is sensitive to inputs *A* and *B*. Note that if any bit within *A* or *B* changes, the procedure will execute. In particular, not all bits of a vector need to change in order to cause a procedure to execute; only one bit changing within a vector causes the procedure to execute.

The procedure uses the assignment statement "*S* <= *A* + *B*;". That statement applies the addition operation, "+", to the two vector ports *A* and *B*. "+" is a built-in arithmetic operator that performs addition on various data types, including vectors. Built-in arithmetic operators include "+", "-", "*", "/", and "%", and "**", for add, subtract, multiply, divide, modulus, and power, respectively. The first four operators should be self-explanatory. The modulus operator means remainder: "*a* % *b*" is the remainder when *a* is divided by *b*, and is thus *0* when *b* divides a exactly. The power operator works as follows: "*a* ** *b*" means *a* raised to the power of *b*, or a^b. The operators are intentionally defined to be similar to the operators in the C programming language.

Figure 4.7 shows a testbench for the simple 4-bit adder of Figure 4.6. The testbench only includes three vectors. A good testbench would instead have many more vectors, would be self-checking, and would add blank lines between vectors (all of which are omitted for reasons of brevity here).

Simulation of the testbench of Figure 4.7 will result in *S_s* first equaling "*0011+0001*", or "*0100*". In other words, 3 + 1 equals 4. After 10 ns, *S_s* will equal "*1100+0011*", or "*1111*". In other words, 12 + 3 equals 15. The vectors need not be specified as binary constants, but could instead be specified as decimal constants to improve readability, as in the last vector. The last vector adds 5 + 2, which should result in *S_s* being "*0111*", or 7.

The above example introduced a 4-bit adder with no carry-in bit and no carry-out bit. Figure 4.8 illustrates a description having carry-in and carry-out bits, *Ci* and *Co*, respectively. The description uses a technique that extends inputs *A* and *B* into 5-bit numbers, adds them and the carry-in to create a 5-bit sum, and then splits that 5-bit sum into a 1-bit carry-out bit and a 4-bit sum output. The language features involved in that technique will now be discussed

```
`timescale 1 ns/1 ns

module Testbench();

   reg [3:0] A_s, B_s;
   wire [3:0] S_s;

   Add4 CompToTest(A_s, B_s, S_s);

   initial begin
      A_s <= 4'b0011; B_s <= 4'b0001;
      #10;
      A_s <= 4'b1100; B_s <= 4'b0011;
      #10;
      A_s <= 4'd5; // Equivalent to 4'b0101
      B_s <= 4'd2; // Equivalent to 4'b0010
      // Good testbench needs more vectors
   end
endmodule
```

Figure 4.7 Simple 4-bit adder testbench.

```
`timescale 1 ns/1 ns

module Add4wCarry(A, B, Ci, S, Co);

   input [3:0] A, B;
   input Ci;
   output [3:0] S;
   reg [3:0] S;
   output Co;
   reg Co;

   reg [4:0] A5, B5, S5;

   always @(A, B, Ci) begin
      A5 = {1'b0, A}; B5 = {1'b0, B};
      S5 = A5 + B5 + Ci;
      S <= S5[3:0];
      Co <= S5[4];
   end
endmodule
```

Figure 4.8 4-bit adder description with carry-in and carry-out.

CONCATENATION

The description in Figure 4.8 uses the concatenation operator. The ***concatenation operator***, "*{ }*", joins bits from two or more expressions, which are separated by commas within the curly brackets. The description concatenates *0* and the 4-bit value of *A*, resulting in a value consisting of the five bits: "*0 A[3] A[2] A[1] A[0]*". Thus if *A* were "*0011*", the result of the concatenation would be "*00011*". As another example of concatenation, *{2b'11, 2b'00, 2b'01}* would yield "*110001*".

Concatenation is needed in the description to compute the carry-out bit. If the description had merely computed the sum as "*S <= A + B + Ci;*", the result would have been the correct 4-bit sum, but the carry-out bit would not have been captured. Instead, the description first converts the 4-bit *A* and *B* operands into 5-bit operands *A5* and *B5* by using the concatenation operator to prepend a *0* to each item. The description then adds *A5 + B5 + Ci* into a 5-bit value *S5*. The fifth bit of *S5*, namely *S5[4]*, will represent the carry-out bit of the 4-bit addition. Finally, the description sets the sum *S* to the lower four bits of *S5*, namely *S5[3:0]*, and sets the carry-out bit *Co* to the fifth bit of *S5*, namely *S5[4]*. Multiple bits within a vector can be accessed using a ***part selection*** by specifying the highest and lowest bits potion within parentheses separated by a colon. For example, *S[3:1]* will result in a 3-bit vector consisting of bits 3, 2, and 1 of the vector *S*.

BLOCKING VERSUS NON-BLOCKING ASSIGNMENTS

The description in Figure 4.8 uses a new type of procedural assignment statement using "=" rather than using "<=". A procedural assignment using the "=" operator is known as a ***blocking assignment statement***. A blocking assignment *updates* the left-side variable with the value of the right-side expression *before proceeding* to execute the next statement. In contrast, a ***non-blocking assignment statement***, which uses the "<=" operator, *schedules an update* of the left-side variable with the value of the right-side expression *and proceeds* to execute the next statement, as was discussed in Chapter 3. Until now, we have been using non-blocking assignment statements. Readers familiar with the C programming language will notice that a blocking assignment is most similar to variable assignment statements in C, in which the variable is updated before execution proceeds.

The three blocking assignment statements in the procedure of Figure 4.8 are used to compute intermediate values needed to determine the sum and carry-out bits for the 4-bit adder. The description in Figure 4.8 first assigns the concatenation of *0* and the 4-bit input *A* to the variable *A5*, and assigns the concatenation of *0* and the 4-bit input *B* to the variable *B5*. Because those assignments are blocking, the description can immediately use the values assigned to *A5* and *B5* to compute the 5-bit sum as *"S5 = A5 + B5 + Ci;"*. By using blocking assignment for the assignment to *S5* also, the description can immediately use the sum value in order to separate it into the final 4-bit sum output, *S*, and the carry-out output, *Co*. If non-blocking assignments had instead been used to assign *A5*, *B5*, and *S5*, the resulting values for *S* and *Co* would be incorrect, as they would be based on whatever the previous values of *A5*, *B5*, and *S5* were.

As a general guideline, blocking assignments should be used for computing intermediate values in order to simplify the code. They are typically used as a coding convenience only, to avoid having overly-complex expressions on the right side of a statement. When used as such, the variables on the left sides will usually synthesize into just wires, not registers.

LEFT-SIDE CONCATENATION

Figure 4.9 shows a simpler 4-bit adder description with carry-in and carry-out, which makes use of concatenation on the left side of an assignment statement, as follows: "*{Co, S} <= A + B + Ci;*". The left side, *{Co, S}*, creates a 5-bit item consisting of the single bit *Co* and the four bits of *S*. Verilog automatically converts the operands of "+" into the widest width of any involved operands, including the left side of an assignment. Thus, the *A*, *B*, and *Ci* variables are automatically converted to five bits each, through automatic padding in which *0*s are prepended to each variable. For example, if *A* were *0011*, *B* were *0001*, and *Ci* were *0*, then the statement would add *00011 + 00001 + 00000* to yield *00100*, with *Co* getting the first *0*, and *S* getting *0100*.

Both descriptions of the 4-bit adder—the one using blocking assignments and the one using left-side concatenation—would synthesize to the same circuit, even though the former description is longer. The latter merely used some of Verilog's automatic conversion features to perform padding and bit assignment automatically.

```
`timescale 1 ns/1 ns

module Add4wCarry(A, B, Ci, S, Co);

   input [3:0] A, B;
   input Ci;
   output reg [3:0] S;
   output reg Co;

   always @(A, B, Ci) begin
      {Co, S} <= A + B + Ci;
   end
endmodule
```

Figure 4.9 Alternative 4-bit adder description with carry-in and carry-out, using left-side concatenation.

```
`timescale 1 ns/1 ns

module Testbench();

   reg [3:0] A_s, B_s;
   reg Ci_s;
   wire [3:0] S_s;
   wire Co_s;

   Add4wCarry CompToTest(A_s, B_s, Ci_s, S_s, Co_s);

   initial begin
      A_s <= 4'b0011; B_s <= 4'b0001;
      Ci_s <= 0;
      #10;
      A_s <= 4'b1100; B_s <= 4'b0011;
      Ci_s <= 1;
      #10;
      A_s <= 4'd5; // Equivalent to 4'b0101
      B_s <= 4'd2; // Equivalent to 4'b0010
      // Good testbench needs more vectors
   end
endmodule
```

Figure 4.10 Testbench for 4-bit adder with carry-in and carry-out.

Figure 4.10 shows a testbench for the 4-bit adder with carry-in and carry-out of Figure 4.8 or Figure 4.9. The testbench only includes a few vectors; as mentioned before, a good testbench would have many more vectors, and would also use self-checking statements to check for correct output. Simulation of the testbench of Figure 4.10 will result in *S_s* first equaling "*0011+0001+0*", or "*0100*", and *Co* will be *0*. In other words, 3 + 1 + 0 equals 5. After 10 ns, *S_s* will equal "*1100+0011+1*", or "*0000*", with *Co* equal to *1*. In other words, 12 + 3 + 1 equals 16. Finally, after another 10 ns, *S_s* will equal "*0101+0010+1", or 1000*" with *Co* of *0*. In other words, 5 + 2 + 1 = 8. Note that the last vectors were written using decimal constants, to show how decimal constants can improve readability.

4.3 SHIFT REGISTERS

Figure 4.1 presented a multifunction register, which included shift left and shift right operations. If one only requires that the input be serially shifted into the register, a simpler shift register description could be created. Figure 4.11(a) shows a simple 4-bit right shift register, with control input *Shr*, data input *Shr_in*, and parallel 4-bit output *Q*. Figure 4.11(b) shows the register's operations. On every clock cycle that the *Shr* control input is *1*, the register shifts the contents one position to the right and loads *Shr_in* into the leftmost bit.

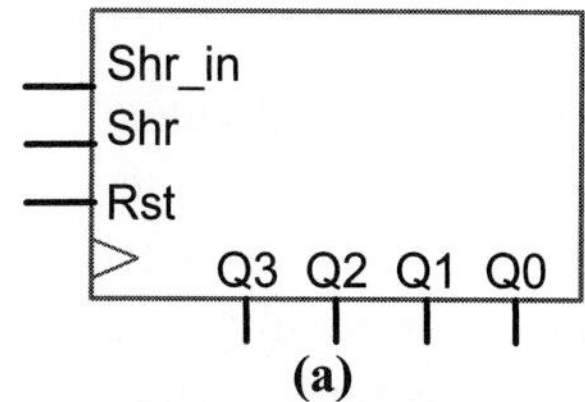

(a)

Shr	Operation
0	Retain Value
1	Shift right

(b)

Figure 4.11 4-bit shift register: (a) block diagram, (b) operation table.

Similar to the multifunction register description of Figure 4.1, the description for the 4-bit shift register in Figure 4.12 declares *R* as a 4-bit reg variable, with that variable being used to store the register contents. The continuous assignment statement *"assign Q = R;"* is used to assign the register contents to the output *Q*. The description performs shifting by assigning the value for each register bit independently as an individual statement, thereby requiring four separate statements to perform the right shift operation. Although such a description is correct, assigning each bit individually results in excessive code for larger registers. For example, a 32-bit shift register would have 32 assignment statements. Not only is such code hard to read, but such code may contain errors due to cut-and-paste-and-revise errors or due to simply typing the wrong bit number in one of those statements.

Alternatively, the shift operation could be achieved by concatenating each bit of the register together using a single assignment statement: *"R <= {Shr_in, R[3], R[2], R[1]};"*. While simpler and more compact than individual assignment statements, using concatenation is still time-consuming and error prone for large items, as one has to manually enter the bits in the proper order. A loop statement can yield a better description.

```
`timescale 1 ns/1 ns

module ShiftReg4(Q, Shr, Shr_in, Clk, Rst);

   output [3:0] Q;
   input Shr, Shr_in;
   input Clk, Rst;

   reg [3:0] R;

   always @(posedge Clk) begin
      if (Rst == 1)
         R <= 4'b0000;
      else if (Shr == 1) begin
         R[3] <= Shr_in; R[2] <= R[3];
         R[1] <= R[2]; R[0] <= R[1];
      end
   end

   assign Q = R;
endmodule
```

Figure 4.12 4-bit shift register.

PROCEDURES WITH FOR LOOP STATEMENTS

Consider a 32-bit version of the shift register of Figure 4.11. Assigning individual bits of the register may be prone to error. For larger register sizes, a simpler description utilizes a *loop* to assign the bits. A ***loop statement*** defines statements that will be executed repeatedly some number of times. Two commonly used types of loops are *for* loops and *while* loops. The following discussion describes *for* loops; *while* loops will be discussed in a later section.

A ***for loop statement*** is typically used to describe a loop whose statements execute a specific number of times. The 32-bit register description of Figure 4.13 illustrates use of a *for* loop. The description declares a variable named *Index* (other names, like *I* or *Count*, would also be valid), commonly called an ***index variable***, that will be used in conjunction with the *for* loop statement to keep count of the number of *for* loop iterations. The *for* loop statement itself consists of three parts, contained in parentheses and separated by semicolons. The first part is the *initialization* part, which is executed only once at the start of the *for* loop's execution. In the figure, the initialization is "*Index=0*". The second part is the *condition* part, which is checked before each loop iteration. If the condition is true, the loop executes its sub-statements. In the figure, the condition part is "*Index<=30*", meaning Index is less than or equal to 30. After the sub-statements execute once, the third part of the *for* loop statement, the *index variable update* part, executes. That part typically updates the index variable. In the figure, the update is "*Index=Index+1*".

```
`timescale 1 ns/1 ns

module ShiftReg32(Q, Shr, Shr_in, Clk, Rst);

   output [31:0] Q;
   input Shr, Shr_in;
   input Clk, Rst;

   reg [31:0] R;
   integer Index;

   always @(posedge Clk) begin
      if (Rst == 1)
         R <= 32'h00000000;
      else if (Shr == 1) begin
         R[31] <= Shr_in;
         for (Index=0; Index<=30; Index=Index+1) begin
            R[Index] <= R[Index+1];
         end
      end
   end
   assign Q = R;
endmodule
```

Figure 4.13 32-bit shift register description using a *for* loop.

The description in Figure 4.13 performs the right shift operation by first assigning the input data *Shr_in* to the leftmost bit of the register contents *R*, using the statement "*R[31] <= Shr_in;*". The remaining lower 31 bits of the register will be assigned using the *for* loop. The loop is declared as "*for (Index=0; Index<=31; Index=Index+1)*". Its sub-statement is a begin-end block having one non-blocking assignment statement, "*R[Index] <= R[Index+1];*". During each iteration of the loop, the assignment statement within the loop will assign to the bit at the current position, *Index*, the value currently stored in the next highest bit location, *Index+1*. For example, if *Index* were currently equal to 2, the statement "*R[index] <= R[index+1];*" would be equivalent to the statement "*R[2] <= R[3];*", which is how the 4-bit shift register description of Figure 4.12 assigned the individual bits. After executing the loop, all bits of the register contents *R* will have been assigned.

The description again uses a continuous assignment statement "*assign Q = R;*" to assign the register contents to the output *Q*.

Note that the loop only iterates from 0 to 30, and not over all bits of the register, 0 to 31. This is because the leftmost, or highest-order, bit gets its value from the input *Shr_in*, and thus need not be assigned within the *for* loop. If the shift register were instead designed to shift left into the register, the *for* loop would instead be declared to iterate from 1 to 31 and to assign the rightmost, or lowest-order, bit using a separate assignment statement.

Although the *for* loop will execute the loop one iteration at a time, during synthesis the *for* loop will be expanded, or unrolled, such that all iterations of the loop will be executed simultaneously (as the assignment statements are non-blocking). For the shift register description, the resulting synthesized circuit would be equivalent to the synthesized hardware circuit had the description specified 32 separate non-blocking assignments, one for each bit of the shift register.

Two new language features appeared in this example, which we now discuss.

INTEGER VARIABLES

The 32-bit register description declared the index variable *Index* as an integer: "*integer Index;*". ***integer*** is another variable data type, representing a positive or negative value up to 32 bits wide. Earlier, the *reg* variable data type was introduced. Strictly speaking, the integer type is not needed in the language, because the reg type could be used instead. The integer type exists to make code more self-documenting, meaning more self-explanatory. The integer type is generally used to represent decimal number quantities that will not become a hardware register. The index variable of a *for* loop is one such quantity, because we expect synthesis to unroll the loop and hence eliminate the index variable from the design.

RELATIONAL, LOGICAL, AND EQUALITY OPERATORS

The 32-bit register description compared the index variable to a constant using the following comparison: "*Index<=30*". The comparison uses the relational operator "<=" that corresponds to "less than or equal to". The operator is identical to the non-blocking assignment operator, which is also "<=". The compiler distinguishes the two operators based on where they are used.

Verilog supports the following built-in relational, logical, and equality operators:

- > : greater than
- < : less than
- >= : greater than or equal
- <= : less than or equal
- *!* : logical negation
- *&&* : logical AND
- || : logical OR
- == : logical equality
- *!=* : logical inequality
- === : logical equality, including *x* and *z* bits
- *!==* : logical inequality, including *x* and *z* bits

Note that the language has logical operators *!*, *&&*, and ||, and has bitwise operators ~, &, and |, which we introduced in Chapter 2. With single bit operands, the logical operators and bitwise operators operate similarly. For example, "*1 && 1*" and "*1 & 1*" both equal *1*. The difference appears when operating on multi-bit vectors. Let 4-bit vectors *A* be *1100* and *B* be *0101*. Then in "*A && B*", the operator treats *A* as true (nonzero) and *B* as true, resulting in "*true && true*" equalling 1 (true). But in "*A & B*", the operator performs a bitwise AND operation *on each corresponding pair of bits*, resulting in *0100*. Logical operators are commonly used in statements with conditional expressions, like *if-else* or *while*. Bitwise operators are more common for describing combinational logic or datapath operations like the bitwise AND operation in an arithmetic-logic unit (ALU).

A partial testbench for the 32-bit shift register appears in Figure 4.14. The testbench first resets the register contents by setting *Rst_s* to *1*, and waits for one clock cycle. Next, the testbench enables the shift operation by setting *Shr_s* to *1,* and sets the data input to *1*. The testbench then waits for sixteen clock cycles, which will result in shifting a total of sixteen *1*s into the register. Instead of writing sixteen *"@(posedge Clk_s);"* delay statements, the testbench also uses a *for* loop, which executes sixteen times over the range 0 to 15 and includes only one delay statement. Because the loop index itself is not used within the *for* loop, that loop could have declared the loop to iterate over any range of size sixteen, such as

```
...
    // Vector Procedure
   initial begin
      Rst_s <= 1;
      Shr_s <= 0; Shr_in_s <= 0;
      @(posedge Clk_s);
      #5 Rst_s <= 0;
      @(posedge Clk_s);
      #5 Shr_s <= 1; Shr_in_s <= 1;
      for (Index=0; Index<=15; Index=Index+1) begin
         @(posedge Clk_s);
      end
      #5;
      if (Q_s != 32'hFFFF0000)
         $display("Failed Q=FFFF0000");
      Shr_s <= 1; Shr_in_s <= 0;
      for (Index=0; Index<=15; Index=Index+1) begin
         @(posedge Clk_s);
      end
      #5;
      if (Q_s != 32'h0000FFFF)
         $display("Failed Q=0000FFFF");
      Shr_s <= 0;
   end
endmodule
```

Figure 4.14 32-bit shift register testbench.

100 to 115, or 2 to 17. However, good practice dictates using a range whose purpose clearly indicates sixteen iterations, such as 0 to 15, or perhaps 1 to 16.

After shifting in sixteen *1*s, the testbench verifies the register's output using a self-check to compare *Q_s* with the expected output value of "*32'hFFFF0000*", displaying "*Failed Q=FFFF0000*" if the self-check fails.

Using a similar approach, the testbench subsequently shifts in sixteen *0*s and verifies the register output using another self-check to compare the register output with the hexadecimal value "*32'h0000FFFF*". The testbench then disables the shift control input by setting *Shr_s* to *0*, before terminating.

[SIMUL] FILE INPUT AND OUTPUT

As designs become more complex and have larger data widths for inputs, outputs, and internal variables, specifying a robust set of test vectors with a testbench can become difficult and time-consuming. Thus, as the number of required test vectors increases, designing testbenches using a large sequence of assignment statements, delay statements, and self-checking statements, may become more difficult. Consider the 32-bit shift register design presented in Figure 4.13 and the corresponding testbench appearing in Figure 4.14. Creating a more robust testbench that shifts into the register several distinct 32-bit values would require hundreds of lines of code. For example, shifting in just one distinct 32-bit test vector would require 64 statements—32 assignment statements assigning the shift data input for each bit, with each assignment followed by a delay statement to wait for the next rising clock edge (we avoided so many statements in the simple testbench of Figure 4.14 by using test vectors consisting of a sequence of just *1*s, then of just *0*s). Defining 100 such vectors would require 64*100 = 6,400 statements.

The approach for testing a module can be improved by reading the test vectors from an input file. A ***file*** is a document located on the host computing system, which can be read from or written by the HDL simulator. Not only does using a file yield a more compact representation of test vectors, but using a file also allows for easy inclusion of new test vectors into an existing test vector file, and allows for use of different files that test different design aspects or scenarios. Furthermore, new vectors can be added to the input file without requiring re-compilation in order to re-simulate.

Figure 4.15 shows a testbench that reads test vectors from a file for the 32-bit shift register of Figure 4.13, showing only the testbench vector procedure. The vector procedure will read several test vectors from the input file, where the vector file specifies the bits that will be shifted into the register during simulation. The description uses several built-in system procedures for accessing files.

Functions and tasks

Verilog supports four types of procedures: the initial construct, the always construct, tasks, and functions. The initial and always procedure types have already been introduced. Those procedure types are enabled at the beginning of simulation, with the initial construct executing once, and the always construct executing repeatedly.

In contrast, tasks and functions are procedures that are called from within a description. A ***function*** is a procedure having at least one argument, returning a value, and not having any time-controlling statements like delay control or event control. A ***task*** is a procedure having any number of arguments (including none), no return value, and possibly containing time-controlling statements. A function may be thought of as a (possibly complex) computation of a value, whereas a task is an activity itself. A function may itself call other functions, but may not call a task (because that task might have time-controlling statements). A task may call either functions or tasks.

The following section will introduce several built-in system tasks and functions to conduct file input and output.

```
   integer FileId;
   reg[8:0] BitChar;
...
   // Vector Procedure
   initial begin
      FileId = $fopen("vectors.txt", "r");
      if (FileId == 0)
         $display("Could not open input file.");
      else begin
         Rst_s <= 1;
         Shr_s <= 0; Shr_in_s <= 0;
         @(posedge Clk_s);
         #5 Rst_s <= 0;
         @(posedge Clk_s);
         #5 Shr_s <= 1;
         while ($feof(FileId) == 0) begin
            BitChar = $fgetc(FileId);
            if (BitChar == "1") begin
               Shr_in_s <= 1;
               @(posedge Clk_s);
            end
            else if (BitChar == "0") begin
               Shr_in_s <= 0;
               @(posedge Clk_s);
            end
         end
         $fclose(FileId);
      end
      Shr_s <= 0;
   end
endmodule
```

Figure 4.15 32-bit shift register testbench with file input.

File input and output procedures

The file-based testbench in Figure 4.15 uses several built-in system tasks and system functions for file input and output:

- The ***$fopen*** system function opens a file for access. Its first argument is the file name, in this case "*vectors.txt*". Its second argument is the access type, which can be "*r*" for read, "*w*" for write, or "*a*" for append, in this case being "*r*". The function returns an integer that identifies the opened file to later file-access procedures. Such identification is necessary because there may be more than one file opened at a given time. If the file could not be opened (perhaps due to being nonexistent or due to incorrect permissions), the function returns *0*.

- The ***$feof*** system function returns *0* if the end of the file, whose identifier is specified as an argument, has not yet been reached.
- The ***$fgetc*** system function returns the next character in the specified file. A valid character is 8 bits wide. However, this function needs a way to indicate that an error occurred during access (e.g, perhaps due to the specified file not being readable). Thus, the function actually returns a 9-bit value. If an error occurred, the returned value will be 111111111 (which is -1 in decimal). Otherwise, the read character will be in the lower 8 bits, with the high-order bit being 0.
- The ***$fclose*** system task closes the specified previously-opened file.

While loops

The testbench uses a *while* loop. A ***while loop statement*** is a loop that continues to execute its statements as long as the loop's condition evaluates to true. In other words, if the condition is true, the loop's sub-statement is executed, and the condition is checked again. The loop's sub-statement is typically a begin-end block containing one or more statements. A *for* loop is typically used when the specific number of iterations is known (e.g., loop 16 times), whereas a *while* is used when the number of iterations is not known (e.g., loop until the end of the file is reached).

The shift register's testbench vector procedure of Figure 4.15 first opens a file by calling the *$fopen* function, before reading or writing to the file. If the open fails, the procedure displays an error message. Otherwise, the procedure resets the register, and then begins a loop that executes as long as the end of the file has not been reached, checked using the *$feof* function. Each loop iteration consists of reading the next character from the file using the *$fgetc* function, and then checking if the character is *1* or *0* and then setting the register to shift in a *1* or *0*. The testbench can thus contain any number of *0*s and *1*s, in any sequence, and they will be read and shifted in on each clock cycle. Note that this testbench is always shifting; a better testbench would support vectors that perform no shift also.

One might wonder why the if-else-if construct was necessary in the testbench, and specifically why the testbench didn't simply shift in the read character using the statement: "*Shr_in_s <= BitChar;*" The reason is because that assignment would not work properly, due to *Shr_in_s* being a bit, but *BitChar* being a 9-bit value holding the ASCII value of the read character. A read *1* would not be *000000001*, but rather the ASCII encoding corresponding to the character *1* (which would happen to be *000110001*, but that's not really relevant). Thus, the if-else-if compares the read character to the character "*1*", and if the comparison returns true, sets the shift input to a *1* bit.

Defining the vectors within the *vectors.txt* file allows easy changes to the simulated behavior of the testbench. For example, consider the case when the contents of *vectors.txt* file is:

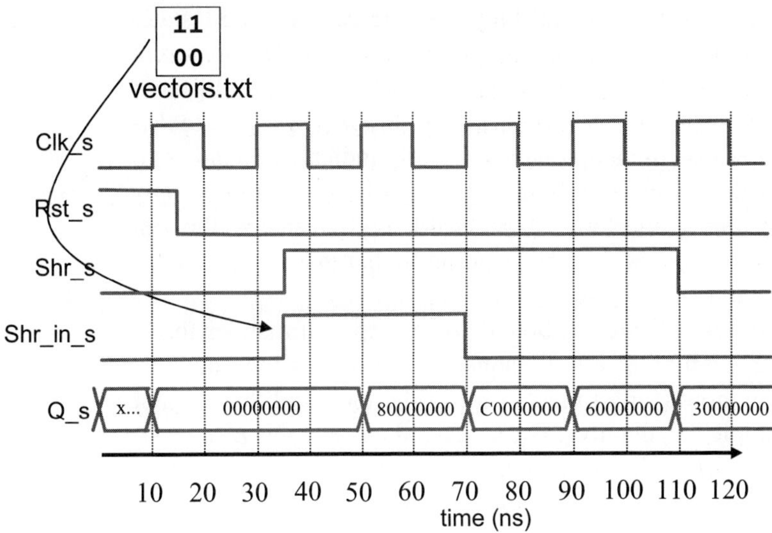

Figure 4.16 32-bit shift register waveform for give vectors.

```
1111111111111111
0000000000000000
```

During simulation, the testbench reads the bits from the file and shifts those bits into the shift register. This input file will first shift sixteen *1*s into the register, followed by sixteen *0*s. The resulting simulation waveform will be identical to the waveform generated from the original testbench that appeared in Figure 4.14.

Figure 4.16 shows the simulation waveform for a 32-bit shift register when the contents of *vectors.txt* are:

```
11
00
```

Notice the four bit values of *1*, *1*, *0*, and *0* being shifted into the register.

[SYNTH] COMMON PITFALL

Creating a loop that cannot be unrolled during synthesis

A common pitfall involves creating an un-synthesizable loop in a description intended for synthesis. In a description intended for synthesis, a loop should be considered merely as a shorthand description for a longer sequence of statements. Consider the *for* loop from Figure 4.13, which is shown again in Figure 4.17(a) for convenience. That loop is a shorthand description for 31 variable assignment statements: "*R[0] <= R[1];*", "*R[1] <= R[2];*", ..., "*R[30] <= R[31];*". A typical synthesis tool would in fact "***unroll***" that *for* loop into the equivalent 31 statements that are shown in Figure 4.17(a). Those statements describe 31 concurrent updates (recall that the order of such statements does not matter) that should occur during a clock cycle of the register that was described in Figure 4.13. The tool is able to unroll the *for* loop because the loop contains clearly indicated bounds of 0 (the lower bound) and 30 (the upper bound). To unroll the loop, the tool simply replicates the loop body 31 times, and for each replicated body instance, the tool replaces the identifier *Index* by the value corresponding to that instance (0 for the first instance, 1 for the second instance, etc.).

A common pitfall is to not indicate the bounds of a loop in a manner that a synthesis tool can readily recognize. If a tool cannot recognize the loop bounds, then the tool does not know how many times to unroll the loop and thus cannot unroll the loop. For example, if the loop were described as "*for (Index=0; Index<=Regwidth; Index<=Index+1)*", and *Regwidth* were declared as anything other than a constant parameter (e.g., as a variable or port), then a synthesis tool might not be able to determine the value of *Regwidth* and thus might not be able to unroll the loop. If an RTL synthesis tool cannot unroll a loop, the tool cannot synthesize the loop.

While loops are also generally not synthesizable, because synthesis tools generally are not able to unroll such loops due to not recognizing the loop bounds. Some synthesis tools are actually able to unroll certain types of *while* loops that are essentially equivalent to *for* loops, such as the while loop in Figure 4.17(b). Assuming that *Index* is declared as an integer variable, a tool might recognize that the *while* loop is equivalent to the *for* loop in Figure 4.17(a), and thus a tool might

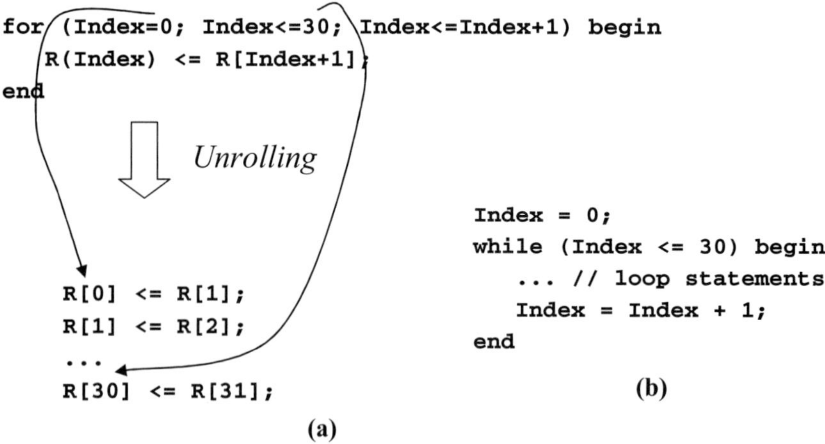

for (Index=0; Index<=30; Index<=Index+1) begin
R(Index) <= R[Index+1]
end
Unrolling
R[0] <= R[1];
R[1] <= R[2];
...
R[30] <= R[31];
(a)
Index = 0;
while (Index <= 30) begin
... // loop statements
Index = Index + 1;
end
(b)

Figure 4.17 Loop unrolling: (a) A loop usually must be un-rollable if the loop is to be synthesized, (b) while loops, even if un-rollable, are best replaced by for loops if intended for synthesis.

unroll the loop. However, because many synthesis tools will not recognize the *while* loop as unrollable, it is best to only use *for* loops with explicit bounds in descriptions intended for synthesis.

Figure 4.14 and Figure 4.15 also used loops. However, whether or not those loops can be unrolled is irrelevant, because those loops appear in a testbench, which will not be synthesized.

4.4 COMPARATORS

An N-bit comparator compares two N-bit numbers *A* and *B* and indicates whether *A* is greater than, less than, or equal to *B*. Creating a behavioral description for either two unsigned numbers, or for two signed numbers, should be straightforward based on earlier discussions. However, creating a behavioral description of a special comparator (used mainly for demonstration purposes here) that compares an unsigned number *A* with a signed number *B,* is not obvious, and thus will be discussed in this section. A block diagram of that comparator appears in Figure 4.18(a). *A* could be 0 to 15 (*0000* to *1111*), while *B* could be -8 to 7 (*1000* to *0111*) The need therefore exists to represent both unsigned and signed numbers.

UNSIGNED AND SIGNED NUMBERS

Section 4.2 presented a behavioral description of a 4-bit adder in which the 4-bit inputs and outputs were unsigned values. In Verilog, input and output ports, and reg variables, are interpreted as unsigned values, unless specified as otherwise.

In this example of a special comparator, whose block diagram appears in Figure 4.18(a), input *A* should be interpreted as unsigned but input *B* should be interpreted as signed. For example, "*1111*" on *A* should be interpreted as +15, while "*1111*" on *B* should be interpreted as -1. Making *B* be interpreted as signed can be accomplished by adding the keyword *signed* after the keyword *input*, as shown in Figure 4.18(b), and as follows: "*input signed [3:0] B;*". The keyword ***signed*** may be added after the keyword *input*, *output*, or *reg*, to cause the values of those data items to be interpreted as signed values.

If both *A* and *B* were signed, no special care would be needed in the rest of the description; the two inputs could simply be compared using the "<" and ">" operators. However, because *A* is unsigned while *B* is signed, special care must be taken when comparing the two numbers. In particular, Figure 4.18(b) shows that *A* must first be converted to a signed number before comparing with *B*. The system function ***$signed*** changes the interpretation of a value from unsigned to signed. However, just using *$signed* alone isn't enough, because the unsigned number may have a *1* in the high-order bit, which represents a negative number in a signed representation.

For example, "*1111*" is +15 when interpreted as unsigned, but is -1 when interpreted as signed. We clearly do not wish to convert +15 into -1 before com-

(a)

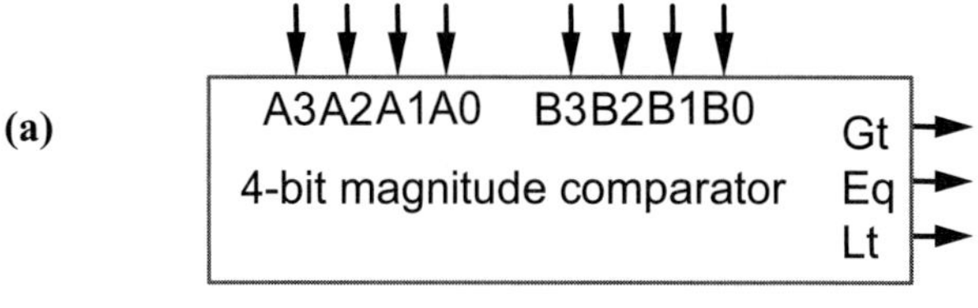

(b)

```
`timescale 1 ns/1 ns

module Comp4(A, B, Gt, Eq, Lt);

   input [3:0] A;
   input signed [3:0] B;
   output Gt, Eq, Lt;
   reg Gt, Eq, Lt;

   always @(A, B) begin
      if ($signed({1'b0,A}) < B) begin
         Gt <= 0; Eq <= 0; Lt <= 1;
      end
      else if ($signed({1'b0,A}) > B) begin
         Gt <= 1; Eq <= 0; Lt <= 0;
      end
      else begin
         Gt <= 0; Eq <= 1; Lt <= 0;
      end
   end
endmodule
```

Figure 4.18 4-bit comparator: (a) block diagram, (b) description using both unsigned and signed types in one module.

paring with *B*; we still want +15. Thus, Figure 4.18(b) first extends the width of *A* from four to five bits with a *0* in the highest-order bit, using the concatenation operator: "*{1'b0,A}*". The 5-bit value is then converted to a signed interpretation: "*$signed({1'b0,A})*". Thus, "*1111*", which is +15, would be converted to "*01111*", before being interpreted as signed, and thus would still be interpreted as +15. That number can then be compared with *B* using the "<" operator, which would involve *B* being automatically extended to five bits also (automatically sign-extended to preserve the sign and correct value).

With the issue of comparing unsigned and signed numbers now resolved, the description simply compares the values of *A* and *B* using an *if-else-if* construct, setting the output values appropriately. For example, if *A* > *B*, the description sets *Gt* to *1* and sets *Eq* and *Lt* to *0*. Note the begin-end blocks in the *if-else-if* construct are required as each of the sub-statements consists of three statements included on a single line. The "good practice" use of begin-end blocks helps to avoid the resulting incorrect behavior if one were to assume the *if-else-if* sub-statements consisted of a single assignment statement.

A testbench for the comparator appears in Figure 4.19. Note that the *reg* variable *B_s* is declared as *signed* because it connects to the comparator module's *B* port, which is signed. The testbench includes vectors that test both positive and negative values of *B*, and includes vectors in which *A* is greater than, less than, and equal to *B*. It also shows how decimal constants can be used to yield more readable vectors.

Note that a negative binary constant can be specified using a *1* in the highest order bit (assuming two's complement representation), as in "*4'b1111*", whereas a negative decimal constant requires a "-" sign in front of the constant, as in "*-4d1*". A good testbench would include many more vectors, and would be self-checking.

COMMON PITFALL

Unintentional use of one of Verilog's many automatic conversions

Verilog contains many automatic conversion rules that are the source of numerous coding mistakes. For example, suppose the designer of the testbench in Figure 4.19 wrote a test vector that used the assignment "*B_s <= -4'd15;*", with the intention being to assign *B_s* the value of -15. However, *B_s* is only 4-bits wide and thus the most negative number it can represent is -8. Rather than report an error, Verilog's automatic conversion rules result in the following. The 4-bit decimal 15 would be represented as "*1111*". The negative of "*1111*" (15) is automatically converted to the 5-bit value "*10001*" (-15), which is five bits because -15 can't be rep-

```
`timescale 1 ns/1 ns

module Testbench();

   reg [3:0] A_s;
   reg signed [3:0] B_s;
   wire Gt_s, Eq_s, Lt_s;

   Comp4 CompToTest(A_s, B_s, Gt_s, Eq_s, Lt_s);

   initial begin
      A_s <= 4'b0011; B_s <= 4'b0001;
      #10 A_s <= 4'b1111; B_s <= 4'b0111;
      #10 A_s <= 4'b0111; B_s <= 4'b1011;
      #10 A_s <= 4'b0001; B_s <= 4'b0010;
      #10 A_s <= 4'b0001; B_s <= 4'b0001;
      #10 A_s <= 4'b0000; B_s <= 4'b1111;
      #10 A_s <= 4'd1; B_s <= -4'd1;
      #10 A_s <= 4'd1; B_s <= -4'd8;
      // Good testbench needs more vectors
   end
endmodule
```

Figure 4.19 4-bit comparator testbench.

resented in four bits. The assignment of this value to the 4-bit *B_s* variable causes the high-order bit to be ignored, making *B_s=0001*. That value is likely not what was intended by the designer, and simulation results will likely be different than expected.

Verilog contains many such automatic conversion rules. The intent was to simplify the job of coding. In some cases the rules do simplify matters, but they also result in many undetected coding mistakes. Avoiding common pitfalls related to conversion is hard. We can simply suggest using great caution and getting in the habit of being as explicit as reasonably possible when coding. When making use of automatic conversions, adding a comment describing that use (e.g., "*// High-order bit ignored*") may help future designers that read your code realize your intent.

4.5 REGISTER FILES

A register file can provide for compact storage when a design contains multiple registers. Register files come in different sizes. A 4x32 register file has 4 registers, each being 32 bits wide. Figure 4.20(a) shows a structural design of a 4x32 register file having what is known as one "write port" and one "read port" (not to be confused with Verilog ports).

The register file design uses two 2x4 decoders with enable. Chapter 2 provided the description of a 2x4 decoder. Adding an enable input, which when *0* causes all decoder outputs to be *0*, would be a simple extension of that description.

The register file design also uses three-state buffers (each buffer shown in the figure actually corresponds to 32 buffers), whose functionality is illustrated in Figure 4.20(b). When the control input is *1*, the buffer passes its data input to its output. However, when the control input is 0, the buffer outputs a special value known as "***high impedance***" and written as ***Z*** or *z*. A wire with a high impedance value essentially appears to be disconnected from other wires to which it is actually connected. The purpose of the three-state buffers is to allow the register outputs to simply be wired together to form a bus, rather than being fed through a large and slow multiplexor before reaching the read port's data output. Such bus wiring works correctly only if the design is such that no more than one register can ever output non-high-impedance values onto the bus. The decoder ensures such behavior.

The register file design in Figure 4.20 also contains a signal-strengthening driver, but we can omit that from a register file description, as such drivers would automatically be inserted by a synthesis tool.

The three-state buffers can be treated as internal parts of the registers. Thus, the register file design would require the design of a 32-bit register component having a load control input and an output enable control input (and having internal three-state buffers). The block diagram and functionality of such a register is shown in Figure 4.21.

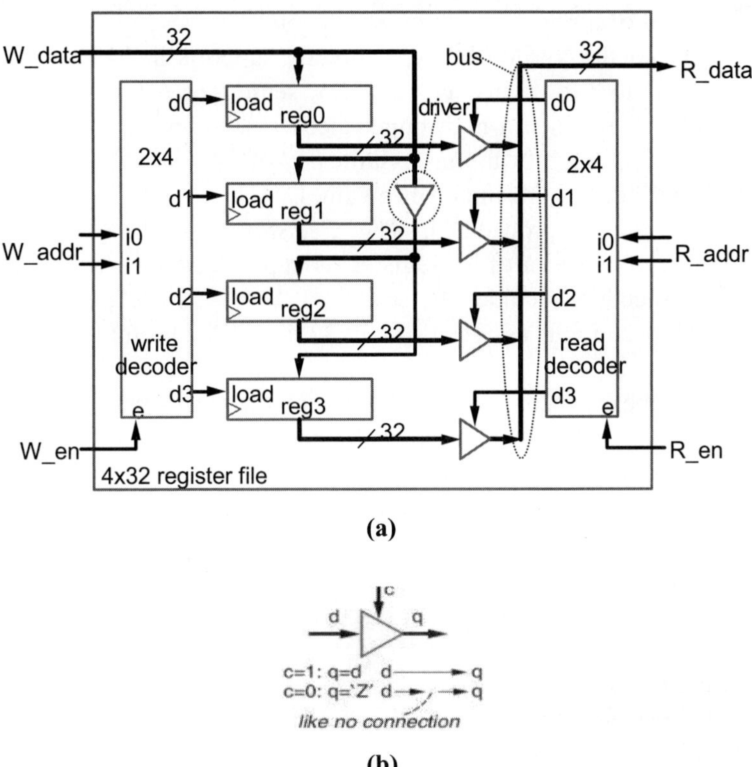

Figure 4.20 Register file: (a) 4x32 register file, (b) functionality of three-state buffers, used to enable wiring together of register outputs.

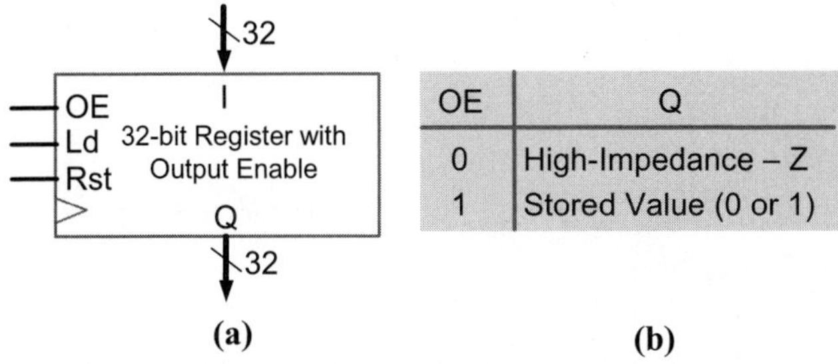

OE	Q
0	High-Impedance – Z
1	Stored Value (0 or 1)

Figure 4.21 Register with output enable: (a) block diagram, (b) output enable functionality.

USING HIGH-IMPEDANCE VALUES

Figure 4.22 provides a description of a register with output enable. The description will make use of the fact that the Verilog bit type directly supports high-impedance values. A bit can be set to *Z* (or *z*) just as it could be set to *0* or *1*. For example, a *reg* variable *S* could be assigned a high-impedance value simply by using the statement "*S* <= *Z*;". A Verilog bit can thus assume any of four values: *0*, *1*, *x* or *X* (undefined value), and *z* or *Z* (high-impedance value).

The description uses two always procedures. The *Register Procedure* describes the main storage and reset behavior of the register, as in previous register descriptions. Note that the procedure includes the statement "*R* <= *32'd0;*", where "*32'd0*" represents 32 *0* bits and thus assigns *0*s to all 32 bits of the vector *R*.

The *Output Procedure* describes the combinational logic of the three-state buffer output behavior of the register. When the output enable input is *1*, the procedure sets the output *Q* to the stored value *R*. When the output enable input is *0*,

```
`timescale 1 ns/1 ns

module Reg32wOE(I, Q, Oe, Ld, Clk, Rst);

   input [31:0] I;
   output [31:0] Q;
   reg [31:0] Q;
   input Oe, Ld;
   input Clk, Rst;

   reg [31:0] R;

   // Register Procedure
   always @(posedge Clk) begin
      if (Rst == 1)
         R <= 32'd0;
      else if (Ld == 1)
         R <= I;
   end

   // Output Procedure
   always @(R, Oe) begin
      if (Oe == 1)
         Q <= R;
      else
         Q <= 32'hZZZZZZZZ;
   end
endmodule
```

Figure 4.22 Description of register with output enable.

the procedure sets the output *Q* to high impedance, or to all *Z*s. The procedure also uses the assignment statement "*Q <= 32'hZZZZZZZZ;*". "*32'hZZZZZZZZ*" represents 32 *Z*s, making the statement equivalent to the statement "*Q <= "ZZZZZZZZZZZZZZZZZZZZZZZZZZZZZZZZ";*" When used in a hexadecimal constant, the *Z* symbol represents four *Z* bits. The *Z* symbol may not be used in a decimal constant.

CONDITIONAL OPERATOR "?"

An alternative, more compact description of the register appears in Figure 4.23. The description replaces the *Output Procedure* by the single continuous assignment statement: "*assign Q = Oe ? R : 32'hZZZZZZZZ;*" The statement uses the operator "*?*", known as the *conditional operator*. The ***conditional operator*** "**?**" is used with three operands as follows: "*A ? B : C*". If *A* is true (non-zero), the operator result is *B*. If *A* is false (zero), the result is *C*. In the figure, "*Q = Oe ? R : 32'hZZZZZZZZ;*" means that if *Oe* is *1*, *Q* gets *R;* if *Oe* is *0*, *Q* gets "*32'hZZZZZZZZ*". The conditional operator is commonly used to replace the simple if-else statement pattern that assigns *Q* in Figure 4.22. However, the operator has additional usefulness because it can appear within expressions, where if-else statements cannot.

A partial testbench for a register with output enable appears in Figure 4.24. The vector procedure enables the register output, performs a load, and checks to

```
`timescale 1 ns/1 ns

module Reg32wOE(I, Q, Oe, Ld, Clk, Rst);

   input [31:0] I;
   output [31:0] Q;
   input Oe, Ld;
   input Clk, Rst;

   reg [31:0] R;

   // Register Procedure
   always @(posedge Clk) begin
      if (Rst == 1)
         R <= 32'd0;
      else if (Ld == 1)
         R <= I;
   end

   assign Q = Oe ? R :  32'hZZZZZZZZ;
endmodule
```

Figure 4.23 Description of register with output enable.

```
...
   // Vector Procedure
  initial begin
     Rst_s <= 1;
     Oe_s <= 1; Ld_s <= 0;
     I_s <= 32'h00000000;
     @(posedge Clk_s);
     #5 Rst_s <= 0;
     @(posedge Clk_s);
     #5 Ld_s <= 1; I_s <= 32'h000000FF;
     @(posedge Clk_s);
     #5;
     if (Q_s !== 32'h000000FF)
        $display("Failed output enabled");
     Ld_s <= 0; Oe_s <= 0;
     #5;
     if (Q_s !== 32'hZZZZZZZZ)
        $display("Failed output disabled");
  end
...
```

Figure 4.24 Partial testbench for register with output enable.

see that the loaded data appears at the register's output. The procedure then disables the register output, and checks that the output value becomes high impedance.

The description uses a new operator, "!==". Verilog support four ***equality operators***. The operators "===" and "!==" do bit-by-bit comparisons of their left and right operands, whose bits may include *x*'s or *z*'s, to compare for equality or inequality, respectively. In contrast, the operators "==" and "!=", which were introduced earlier for equality and inequality, respectively, would return *x* (the unknown value) if an operand contains an *x* or *z*. "===" and "!==" never return *x*.

Given this description of a register with output enable, the register file structural design of Figure 4.20 could be described using the earlier-discussed structural description method of instantiating and connecting components. Such a description would instantiate two decoders with enable, and four registers with output enable. The description would connect those components with each other and with external inputs and outputs, as depicted in the circuit of Figure 4.20(a). Such a structural description of a register file appears in Figure 4.25.

```
`timescale 1 ns/1 ns

module RegFile4x32(R_Addr,W_Addr,R_en,W_en,R_Data,W_Data,Clk,Rst);

   input [1:0] R_Addr, W_Addr;
   input R_en, W_en;
   output [31:0] R_Data;
   input [31:0] W_Data;
   input Clk, Rst;

   wire W_d3, W_d2, W_d1, W_d0;
   wire R_d3, R_d2, R_d1, R_d0;

   Dcd2x4wEn R_Dcd (R_Addr[1],R_Addr[0],R_en,
                    R_d3,R_d2,R_d1,R_d0);
   Dcd2x4wEn W_Dcd (W_Addr[1],W_Addr[0],W_en,
                    W_d3,W_d2,W_d1,W_d0);

   Reg32wOE Reg0 (W_Data,R_Data,R_d0,W_d0,Clk,Rst);
   Reg32wOE Reg1 (W_Data,R_Data,R_d1,W_d1,Clk,Rst);
   Reg32wOE Reg2 (W_Data,R_Data,R_d2,W_d2,Clk,Rst);
   Reg32wOE Reg3 (W_Data,R_Data,R_d3,W_d3,Clk,Rst);
endmodule
```

Figure 4.25 Structural description of a 4x32 register file.

[SIMUL] MULTIPLE DRIVERS OF ONE NET

The previous section created a description in which certain nets had multiple drivers. A ***driver*** is the name for the item that provides the net with its value, such as a continuous assignment statement, or the output of a gate. In earlier sections, each net had only one driver. In Figure 4.25, however, the output net *R_Data* has four drivers—one from *Reg0*'s *Q* output port, one from *Reg1*, one from *Reg2*, and one from *Reg3*. Of course, care was taken to ensure that only one output port at a time could drive a value of *0* or *1*, with the other ports driving *Z*. Nevertheless, the net at any time will have four values being written to it, three of which will be *Z*s, and the fourth of which might be *0*, *1*, or *Z*. The simulator must have a method for ***resolving*** these multiple driven values of a net, meaning to translate the multiple values into a single value for the net. The rules for resolving values of a bit are as follows:

- *0* and *z* becomes *0*
- *1* and *z* becomes *1*
- *z* and *z* becomes *z*
- *0* and *1* becomes *x*

- Note: Other resolutions also defined, *0* and *0* becomes *0*, and *1* and *1* becomes *1*, but we should not allow those situations to happen

The most relevant point is that a single *0* or a single *1* driven onto a net, along with any number of *Zs*, will stay as *0* or *1*, respectively; the *Zs* do not interfere with that single *0* or *1*.

Figure 4.26 shows a testbench vector procedure for the register file. The procedure first resets the register file. Using a *for* loop, the procedure then writes some values into each register of the register file, in this case writing 0 to address 0, 1 to address 1, 2 to 2, and 3 to 3. Using a second *for* loop, the procedure reads each register and displays an error message if the read data differs from the expected value. Note that the comparison operator used is "*!==*", not "*!=*". Finally, the procedure checks that the register file outputs all *Zs* when reading is disabled.

```
// Vector Procedure
 initial begin
    Rst_s <= 1;
    R_Addr_s <= 0'b00; W_Addr_s <= 0'b00;
    R_en_s <= 0; W_en_s <= 0;
    @(posedge Clk_s);
    #5 Rst_s <= 0;
    @(posedge Clk_s);
    #5;
    // Write values to registers
    for (Index=0; Index<=3; Index=Index+1) begin
       W_Addr_s <= Index; W_Data_s <= Index;
       W_en_s <= 1;
       @(posedge Clk_s);
       #5;
    end
    W_en_s <= 0;
    // Check for correct read values from registers
    for (Index=0; Index<=3; Index=Index+1) begin
       R_Addr_s <= Index; R_en_s <= 1;
       @(posedge Clk_s);
       #5;
       if( R_Data_s !== Index )
          $display("Failed case %d.", Index);
    end
    R_en_s <= 0;
    #5;
    if( R_Data_s !== 32'hZZZZZZZZ )
       $display("Failed no read case.");
 end
```

Figure 4.26 Vector procedure for a register file testbench.

ARRAYS

As was the case for several other components, the register file can be described behaviorally rather than structurally. A behavioral description appears in Figure 4.27. The description includes the following declaration: "*reg [31:0] RegFile [0:3];*". The "*[0:3]*" declares *RegFile* to be an ***array***, which is a sequence of elements of identical data type. An array of variables or nets can be declared by specifying the ***array element address range*** after the net or reg variable declaration. This particular array declaration is for an array of four elements, whose indices are numbered from 0 to 3 (meaning 0, 1, 2, and 3). Each element is a 32-bit reg variable. An array element is accessed using an index. For example, the reset portion of the description sets the first array element to *0*s using the statement "*RegFile[0] <= 32'd0;*". In that statement, the index is *0*. The description then sets the second, third, and fourth elements using similar statements, having indices of 1, 2, and 3.

```
`timescale 1 ns/1 ns

module RegFile4x32(R_Addr, W_Addr, R_en, W_en,
                   R_Data, W_Data, Clk, Rst);

   input [1:0] R_Addr, W_Addr;
   input R_en, W_en;
   output reg [31:0] R_Data;
   input [31:0] W_Data;
   input Clk, Rst;

   reg [31:0] RegFile [0:3];

   // Write procedure
   always @(posedge Clk) begin
      if (Rst==1) begin
         RegFile[0] <= 32'd0;
         RegFile[1] <= 32'd0;
         RegFile[2] <= 32'd0;
         RegFile[3] <= 32'd0;
      end
      else if (W_en==1) begin
         RegFile[W_Addr] <= W_Data;
      end
   end

   // Read procedure
   always @* begin
      if (R_en==1)
         R_Data <= RegFile[R_Addr];
      else
         R_Data <= 32'hZZZZZZZZ;
   end
endmodule
```

Figure 4.27 Behavioral description of a 4x32 register file.

The description consists of two procedures. The *Write Procedure* handles writes to the register, as well as the reset behavior, which sets each register to *0*s. During a normal write, the *RegFile* array index is not a constant as above, but is instead the value of the input port *W_Addr*, which is a 4-bit vector. Note that a vector may be used to index an array.

The second procedure is the *Read Procedure*, which handles reading of the register file. When read is enabled, the procedure sets the output to the array element corresponding to the read address. When read is disabled, the procedure sets the output to *Z*s. Note that this procedure uses the implicit event control expression notation, "@*", which was defined in Chapter 2. An explicit event control expression would have required listing every element of *RegFile*, namely *RegFile[0]*, *RegFile[1]*, *RegFile[2]*, and *RegFile[3]* (in addition to *R_Addr*), because Verilog does not allow an array itself to appear in an event control expression. While possible for this small register file, explicit listing would become cumbersome for larger register files.

COMMON PITFALL

Confusing bitwise and logical operators

A common mistake is to use bitwise operators where logical operators are intended, or vice-versa. Consider the bitwise and logical AND operators, "&" and "&&". Figure 4.28(a) shows a description that checks if the third bit of *A* is *1* by using bitwise AND "&", setting *BitSet* to *1* if so and to *0* otherwise. Figure 4.28(b) shows the same description, except using logical AND rather than bitwise AND. The description compiles and simulates without error or warning, but sets *BitSet* to *1* whenever *A* is nonzero.

Such errors can be very difficult to find. Avoiding the pitfall requires great care to use the proper operand. Comments may help. When a description doesn't work as expected, experienced designers often check for correct logical versus bitwise operator usage right away.

```
if( A & 4'b0100 ) begin
   BitSet <= 1;
end
else begin
   BitSet <= 0;
end
```

(a)

```
if( A && 4'b0100 ) begin
   BitSet <= 1;
end
else begin
   BitSet <= 0;
end
```

(b)

Figure 4.28 Common pitfall of bitwise operator confusion: (a) desired behavior sets *BitSet* to *1* if *A*'s third bit is *1*, (b) accidental use of logical AND sets *BitSet* to *1* when

CHAPTER 5

Register-Transfer Level (RTL) Design

5.1 HIGH-LEVEL STATE MACHINE (HLSM) BEHAVIOR

Register-transfer level (RTL) design involves describing the behavior of a design as the transfers that occur between registers every clock cycle. One method for such description uses a high-level state machine (HLSM) computation model. The finite-state machine (FSM) model of Chapter 3 allows only Boolean operations and conditions in states and transitions. In contrast, the HLSM model allows arithmetic operations and conditions, such as the addition or comparison of two 8-bit binary numbers. Furthermore, the HLSM model allows explicit declaration of registers, which may be written to and read from in the HLSM's states and transitions.

Figure 5.1 shows an FSM and an HLSM model for the three-cycles-high laser timer system of Section 3.2, whose behavior is such that when a button press is detected, the system holds an output high for exactly three clock cycles. Figure 5.1(a) shows an FSM description of the system, which uses three states to hold the output high for three cycles. However, what if the system was supposed to hold its output high for 512 cycles rather than just three cycles? Creating an FSM with 512 states to hold the output high would result in an unnecessarily large description. For such a system, a high-level state machine model would be more appropriate. Figure 5.1(b) shows a description having identical behavior with the FSM description of Figure 5.1(a) but achieved using a high-level state machine model. The HLSM has only two states, and explicitly declares a 2-bit register *Cnt*. The register *Cnt* is used to count the number of cycles for which the output has been

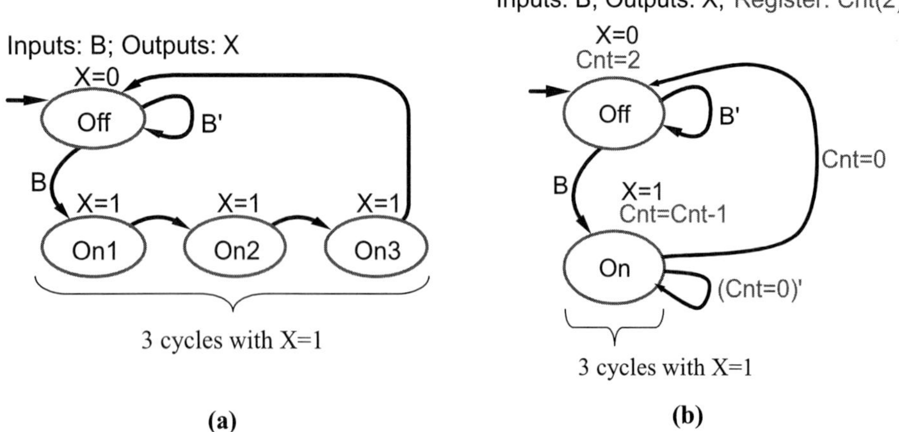

Figure 5.1 Two state machine description types: (a) FSM, (b) high-level state machine (HLSM).

held high. The first state initializes *Cnt* to 2. After a button press has been detected, the second state holds the output high while comparing *Cnt* to *0* and also decrementing *Cnt*. The net result is that the output will be held high for three clock cycles. Initializing *Cnt* to 511 (and also declaring *Cnt* to be a 9-bit register rather than just 2-bits) would result in holding the output high for 512 cycles.

Describing an HLSM in Verilog can be achieved using a straightforward approach similar to the approach for describing an FSM. Similar to the approach for an FSM, the approach for an HLSM considers the target architecture consisting of a combinational logic part and a register part, as shown in Figure 5.2. The earlier-introduced FSM register part consisted only of a state register. The HLSM register part consists of a state register, and of any explicitly declared registers. The figure shows the architecture for the laser timer example system, which has one explicitly declared register, *Cnt*.

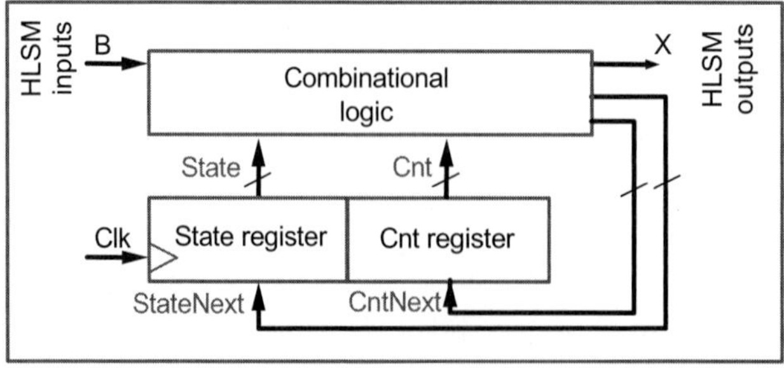

Figure 5.2 Target architecture for an HLSM, consisting of a combinational logic part, and a register part.

```
`timescale 1 ns/1 ns

module LaserTimer(B, X, Clk, Rst);

   input B;
   output reg X;
   input Clk, Rst;

   parameter S_Off = 0,
             S_On  = 1;

   reg [0:0] State, StateNext;
   reg [1:0] Cnt, CntNext;

   // CombLogic
   always @(State, Cnt, B) begin
      ...
   end

   // Regs
   always @(posedge Clk) begin
      ...
   end
endmodule
```

Figure 5.3 Code template for describing the laser timer's HLSM in Verilog.

Describing an HLSM in Verilog follows straightforwardly from the target architecture, as illustrated in Figure 5.3. The description consists of two procedures, one for the combinational logic and one for the registers. In addition to declaring current and next variables for the state register as for an FSM, the description also declares current and next variables for each explicitly declared register in the HLSM. For the laser timer example's one explicit register *Cnt*, the description declares two variables, *Cnt* and *CntNext*.

Figure 5.4 shows the procedure for the combinational logic part of the HLSM. The always procedure is sensitive to all the inputs of the combinational logic. Figure 5.2 shows those inputs to be the values coming from the registers, namely *State* and *Cnt*, and the external input *B*. The procedure consists of a case statement that executes the actions and transitions associated with the current state. Figure 5.1(b) shows those actions to be not just the setting of the HLSM's external outputs (e.g., "*X=0*"), but also setting of explicitly declared registers (e.g., "*Cnt=2*"). The actions in the procedure of Figure 5.4 therefore include not only setting of the external output values (e.g., "*X <= 0;*"), but also setting of the next values for explicitly defined registers (e.g., "*CntNext <= 2;*").

```
...
   reg [0:0] State, StateNext;
   reg [1:0] Cnt, CntNext;

   // CombLogic
   always @(State, Cnt, B) begin
      case (State)
         S_Off: begin
            X <= 0;
            CntNext <= 2;
            if (B == 0)
               StateNext <= S_Off;
            else
               StateNext <= S_On;
         end
         S_On: begin
            X <= 1;
            CntNext <= Cnt - 1;
            if (Cnt == 0)
               StateNext <= S_Off;
            else
               StateNext <= S_On;
         end
      endcase
   end
...
```

Note: Writes are to "next" variable, reads are from "current" variable. See target architecture to understand why.

Figure 5.4 HLSM combinational part.

Note from the architecture shown in Figure 5.2 that for an explicitly declared register, the combinational logic reads the current variable (*Cnt*) but writes the next variable (*CntNext*) for the *Cnt* register. This dichotomy explains why the action "*Cnt <= Cnt - 1*" of the HLSM in Figure 5.1(b) is described in the procedure of Figure 5.4 as "*CntNext <= Cnt - 1;*". Reading is from *Cnt*, while writing is to *CntNext*. When describing HLSMs in an HDL, care must be taken to ensure that reads are from current variables and writes are to next variables for explicitly declared registers.

The transitions in the procedure in Figure 5.4, when reading from an explicitly declared register, must read from the current variable and not the next variable, again based on the target architecture of Figure 5.2. Thus, the transition that detects *Cnt=0* appears as "*Cnt == 0;*".

Figure 5.5 shows the procedure for the register part of the HLSM. The register part actually describes two registers—the state register (involving variables *State* and *StateNext*), and the *Cnt* register (involving variables *Cnt* and *CntNext*). When the clock is rising and reset is not asserted, the procedure updates each current variable with the corresponding next variable. If instead reset were asserted, the procedure sets each current variable to an initial value. Note that the procedure resets *Cnt* to an initial value (*0*), even though such reset behavior is not strictly

```
...
   // Regs
   always @(posedge Clk) begin
      if (Rst == 1 ) begin
         State <= S_Off;
         Cnt <= 0;
      end
      else begin
         State <= StateNext;
         Cnt <= CntNext;
      end
   end
...
```

Figure 5.5 HLSM register part.

necessary for correct functioning of the HLSM, because the HLSM will initialize *Cnt* to *2* in its first state. Such reset behavior was included to follow the modeling guidelines described in Chapter 3, where it was stated that all registers should have defined reset behavior.

Figure 5.6 provides simulation waveforms generated when using the laser timer example testbench introduced in Chapter 3. Note first that the three-cycle-high behavior is identical to the FSM behavior from Chapter 3. The waveforms show two internal variables, *Cnt* and *State*. Note how the system enters state *S_On* on the first rising clock after *B* becomes *1*, causing *Cnt* to be initialized to *2*. *Cnt* is then decremented on each rising clock while in state *S_On*. After *Cnt* reaches *0*, *State* changes to *S_Off*. Note that *Cnt* also was decremented at that time, causing *Cnt* to wrap around from *0* to *3* (*"00" - 1 = "11"*), but that value of *3* was never used, because state *S_Off* sets *Cnt* to *2* again.

Examining the reset behavior of the system is useful. At the beginning of simulation, *Cnt* is unknown. At the first rising clock, *Cnt* is reset to *0* by the description's explicit reset behavior. At the next rising clock, *Cnt* is set to *2* by state *S_Off*.

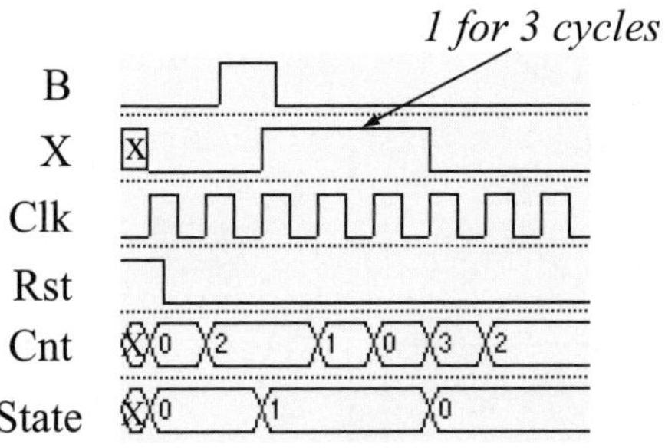

Figure 5.6 HLSM simulation results.

5.2 TOP-DOWN DESIGN— HLSM TO CONTROLLER AND DATAPATH

Recall from Chapters 2 and 3 that top-down design involves first capturing and simulating the behavior of a system, and then transforming that behavior to structure and simulating again. Top-down design divides the design problem into two steps. The first step is to get the behavior right (freed from the complexity of designing structure), and the second step is to derive a structural implementation for that behavior. Dividing into two steps can make the design process proceed more smoothly than trying to directly capture structure. The two-step approach also enables the use of automated tools that automatically convert the behavior to structure.

At the register-transfer level, top-down design involves converting a high-level state machine (HLSM) to a structural design consisting of a controller and a datapath, as shown in Figure 5.7. The datapath carries out the arithmetic operations involved in the HLSM's actions and conditions. The controller sequences those operations in the datapath. The controller itself will be an implementation of an FSM.

The first step in converting an HLSM to a controller and datapath is typically to design a datapath that is capable of implementing all the arithmetic operations of the HLSM. Figure 5.8 shows a datapath capable of implementing the arithmetic operations of the laser timer HLSM.

The datapath includes a register *Cnt*, a decrementer to compute *Cnt-1*, and a comparator to detect when *Cnt* is *0*. Those components are connected to enable the operations needed by the HLSM, with a mux in front of the *Cnt* register to account for the fact that *Cnt* can be loaded from two different sources. The datap-

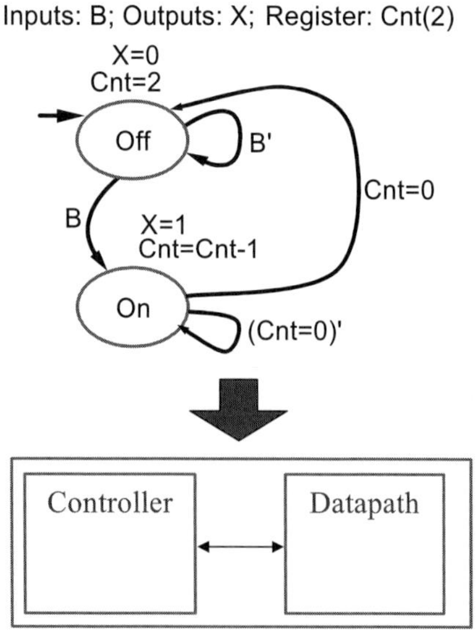

Figure 5.7 RTL top-down design converts an HLSM to a controller and datapath.

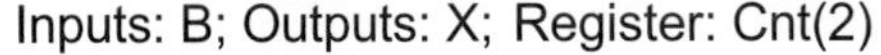

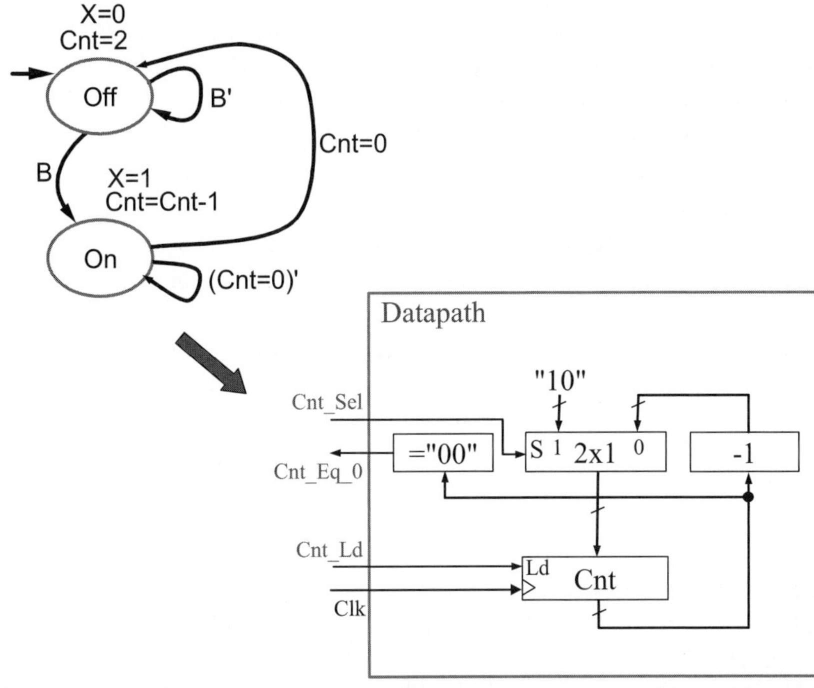

Figure 5.8 Deriving a datapath for the arithmetic operations for the laser timer HLSM.

ath provides clear names for the input and output control signals of the datapath (*Cnt_Sel*, *Cnt_Eq_0*, and *Cnt_Ld*).

After creating a datapath, the next step is to derive a controller by replacing the HLSM with an FSM having the same state and transition structure, but replacing arithmetic operations by Boolean operations that use the datapath input and output control signals to carry out the desired arithmetic operations inside the datapath. Such an FSM is shown in Figure 5.9. The FSM does not contain an explicit register declaration for *Cnt*, as that register now appears in the datapath. Likewise, any writes of that register have been replaced by writes to datapath control signals that configure the input to the register and enable a register load. For example, the assignment "*Cnt = 2*" in state *Off* has been replaced by the Boolean actions "*Cnt_Sel=1*", which configures the datapath mux to pass "*10*" (2) through the mux, and "*Cnt_Ld=1*", which enables loading of the *Cnt* register.

Proceeding with top-down design requires describing Figure 5.9's controller and datapath in Verilog. One option would be to create a module for the controller and a module for the datapath, and then instantiating and connecting a controller module and a datapath module in another higher-level module. However, a simpler approach describes the controller and datapath as procedures within a single module. The simpler approach will now be discussed.

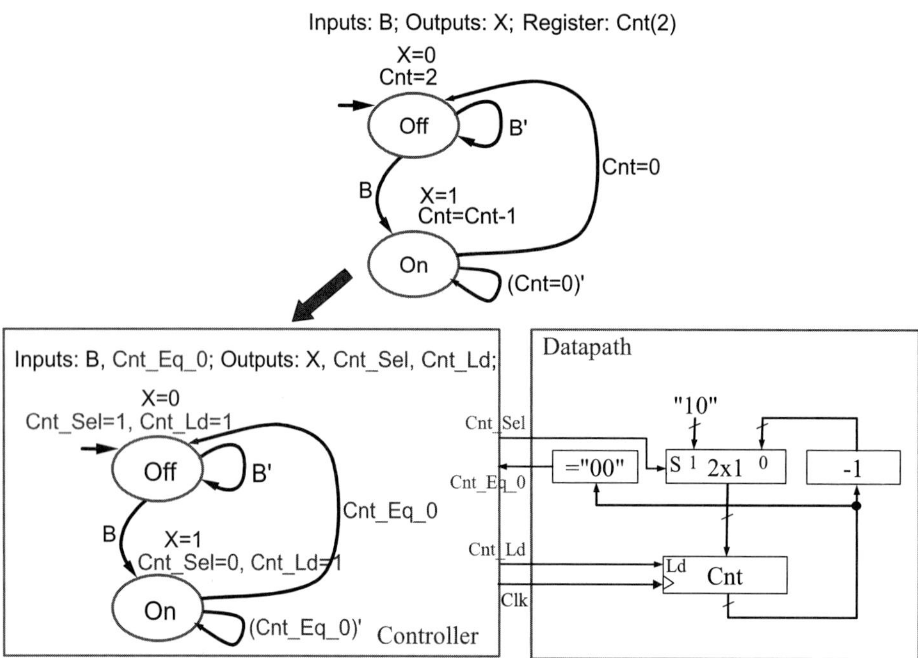

Figure 5.9 Deriving a controller by replacing the HLSM with an FSM that uses the datapath to carry out arithmetic operations.

The datapath itself could be described structurally. Such a description would instantiate four modules: a register, a comparator, a mux, and a decrementer. The description would connect those four components. Each component would require further description as its own module.

The datapath could instead be described behaviorally. Recall from Chapters 2 and 3 that behavioral descriptions are typically easier to create and to understand than structural descriptions. Of course, a behavioral description would need to be further converted to structure to ultimately achieve an implementation, meaning that top-down design must be applied in a hierarchical manner.

One approach to behaviorally describing the datapath involves partitioning the datapath into a combinational logic part and a register part, as shown in Figure 5.10. Notice the similarity of this architecture with the previous architecture in Figure 5.2, which also consists of a combinational logic part and a register part.

Describing the datapath thus proceeds in the same manner as for that previous architecture, namely using two procedures, one for any combinational logic, and one for any registers. Such a two-procedure behavioral description of the datapath is shown in Figure 5.11.

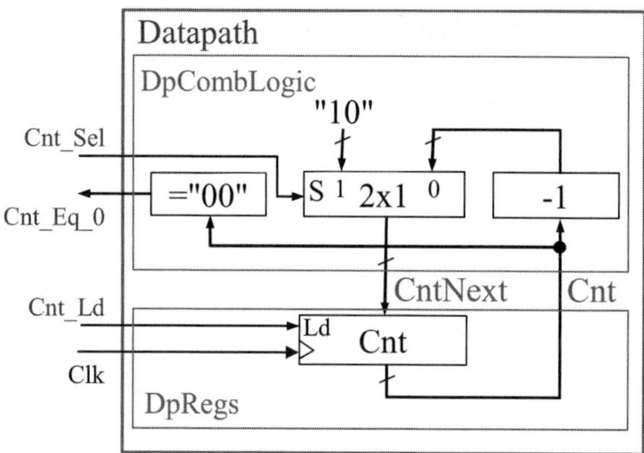

Figure 5.10 Partitioning a datapath into a combinational logic part, and a register part.

The first procedure in Figure 5.11 describes the datapath's combinational logic, whose inputs can be seen from Figure 5.10 to be *Cnt_Sel* and *Cnt*, which therefore appear in the procedure's sensitivity list. In the body of the procedure, the *if-else* statement describes the behavior of the datapath output *CntNext*, including the behavior of the decrementer and the 2x1 mux. The last statement describes the behavior of the datapath output *Cnt_Eq_0*, essentially just describing a comparator with *0*. Notice that those two statements could have appeared in opposite order but would have still described the same behavior.

The second procedure in Figure 5.11 describes the datapath's register. When the clock is rising and the register load input is asserted, the procedure updates the current variable value with the next value. Notice that reset behavior is included for the register, even though such behavior isn't strictly necessary for the correct operation of this particular datapath operation. The reset was included to follow good modeling practice, which involves always including reset behavior for every register. Also notice that only the *Clk* input appears in the procedure's sensitivity list, as the register is synchronous and thus is only updated on (rising) clock edges.

The controller's FSM would also be described using two procedures, one for the combinational part, and one for the register, as was done in Chapter 3, and as shown in Figure 5.12.

Therefore, the controller and datapath description consists of four procedures, two for the datapath (one for combinational logic, one for registers), and two for the controller (one for combinational logic, and one for registers), as shown in Figure 5.13. Those four procedures appear in a single module. The datapath procedures and controller procedures communicate through the variables *Cnt_Eq_0*, *Cnt_Sel*, and *Cnt_Ld*. The other variables are declared either for exclusive use of the datapath (*Cnt*, *CntNext*) or the controller (*State*, *StateNext*).

```
...
   // Shared variables
   reg Cnt_Eq_0, Cnt_Sel, Cnt_Ld;
   // Controller variables
   reg [0:0] State, StateNext;
   // Datapath variables
   reg [1:0] Cnt, CntNext;

   // ------ Datapath Procedures ------ //
   // DP CombLogic
   always @(Cnt_Sel, Cnt) begin
      if (Cnt_Sel==1)
         CntNext <= 2;
      else
         CntNext <= Cnt - 1;

      Cnt_Eq_0 <= (Cnt==0)?1:0;
   end

   // DP Regs
   always @(posedge Clk) begin
      if (Rst == 1 )
         Cnt <= 0;
      else if (Cnt_Ld==1)
         Cnt <= CntNext;
   end
...
```

Figure 5.11 Two-procedure description of a datapath.

```
...
   // ------ Controller Procedures ------ //
   // Ctrl CombLogic
   always @(State, Cnt_Eq_0, B) begin
      case (State)
         S_Off: begin
            X <= 0; Cnt_Sel <= 1; Cnt_Ld <= 1;
            if (B == 0)
               StateNext <= S_Off;
            else
               StateNext <= S_On;
         end
         S_On: begin
            X <= 1; Cnt_Sel <= 0; Cnt_Ld <= 1;
            if (Cnt_Eq_0 == 1)
               StateNext <= S_Off;
            else
               StateNext <= S_On;
         end
      endcase
   end

   // Ctrl Regs
   always @(posedge Clk) begin
      if (Rst == 1 ) begin
         State <= S_Off;
      end
      else begin
         State <= StateNext;
      end
   end
...
```

Figure 5.12 Two-procedure controller description.

```
...
module LaserTimer(B, X, Clk, Rst);
   ...

   parameter S_Off = 0,
             S_On  = 1;

   // Shared variables
   reg Cnt_Eq_0, Cnt_Sel, Cnt_Ld;
   // Controller variables
   reg [0:0] State, StateNext;
   // Datapath variables
   reg [1:0] Cnt, CntNext;

   // ------ Datapath Procedures ------ //
   // DP CombLogic
   always @(Cnt_Sel, Cnt) begin
      ...
   end

   // DP Regs
   always @(posedge Clk) begin
      ...
   end

   // ------ Controller Procedures ------ //
   // Ctrl CombLogic
   always @(State, Cnt_Eq_0, B) begin
      ...
   end

   // Ctrl Regs
   always @(posedge Clk) begin
      ...
   end
endmodule
```

Figure 5.13 Controller and datapath descriptions, consisting of two procedures for the datapath, and two for the controller.

5.3 DESCRIBING A STATE MACHINE USING ONE PROCEDURE

Section 5.1 described how to describe a high-level state machine using two procedures, using one procedure for combinational logic, and a second procedure for registers, as summarized in Figure 5.14(a). The two-procedure description required two variables for each register, a current variable, and a next variable.

A one-procedure description of a high-level state machine is also possible, and is quite commonly used. A one-procedure description is highlighted in Figure 5.14(b). In addition to using only one procedure, the description uses only one variable per register, rather than two variables per register. A one-procedure description thus has advantages of simpler code with clear grouping of related functionality into one procedure. But, as we'll see shortly, the one-procedure description slightly changes the timing behavior.

Figure 5.15 provides a complete one-procedure description of the HLSM for the earlier laser-timer example. The procedure is sensitive only to a rising clock edge. The procedure checks whether the reset input is asserted, in which case the procedure resets all registers (the state register, and explicitly declared registers in the HLSM). If the reset is not asserted, then the procedure executes the HLSM's state actions based on the state variable's value, and sets the next state variable value according to the HLSM transitions.

```
...
module LaserTimer(B, X, Clk, Rst);
...
   reg [0:0] State, StateNext;
   reg [1:0] Cnt, CntNext;

   // CombLogic
   always @(State, Cnt, B) begin
      ...
   end

   // Regs
   always @(posedge Clk) begin
      ...
   end
endmodule
```

(a)

```
...
module LaserTimer(B, X, Clk, Rst);
...
   reg [0:0] State;
   reg [1:0] Cnt;

   always @(posedge Clk) begin
   end
endmodule
```

(b)

Figure 5.14 Alternative approaches for describing a high-level state machine: (a) two-procedure description, (b) one-procedure description.

```
...
module LaserTimer(B, X, Clk, Rst);
   ...
   parameter S_Off = 0,
             S_On  = 1;

   reg [0:0] State;
   reg [1:0] Cnt;

   always @(posedge Clk) begin
      if (Rst == 1 ) begin
         State <= S_Off;
         Cnt <= 0;
      end
      else begin
         case (State)
            S_Off: begin
               X <= 0;
               Cnt <= 2;
               if (B == 0)
                  State <= S_Off;
               else
                  State <= S_On;
            end
            S_On: begin
               X <= 1;
               Cnt <= Cnt - 1;
               if (Cnt == 0)
                  State <= S_Off;
               else
                  State <= S_On;
            end
         endcase
      end
   end
endmodule
```

Figure 5.15 One-procedure description of a laser timer HLSM.

Compared to the two-procedure description shown in Figure 5.4 and Figure 5.5, the one-procedure description in Figure 5.15 is clearly simpler and easier to read. Why then was a two-procedure description introduced? The main reason relates to timing. The one-procedure description of Figure 5.15 does not exactly match the timing of the HLSM in Figure 5.1(b). In particular, the intended HLSM's behavior is such that changes to the HLSM inputs (i.e., to input *B*) would be seen by the HLSM immediately, and thus a change could influence the next state on the rising clock edge immediately following the change. Such behavior is accurately reflected by the two-procedure description, as shown in the waveforms

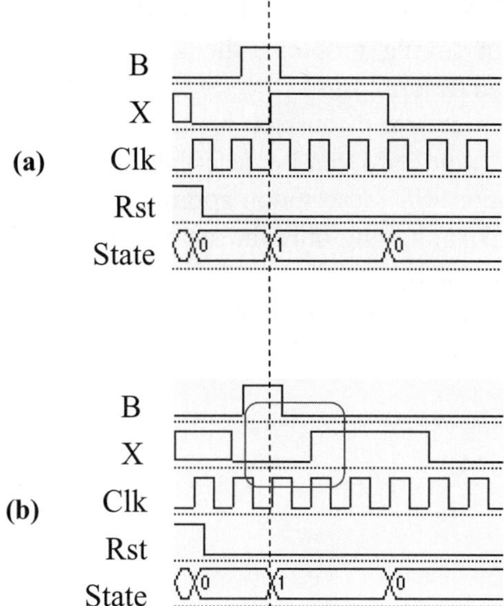

Figure 5.16 Timing differences between different descriptions: (a) In the two-procedure description, a change in *B* appearing sufficiently before a rising clock edge sets up the next state according to the new value of *B*, (b) In the one-procedure synchronous description, *B*'s value is only checked on rising clock edges, and thus a change in *B* is not noticed until the next rising edge, meaning the new value of *B* doesn't impact the next state until *two* rising clock edges after *B* changes.

of Figure 5.16(a), because the combinational logic procedure is independent of the clock input. In contrast, the one-procedure description of Figure 5.15 is synchronous, meaning the procedure only checks the value of *B* on a rising clock edge, and thus a change cannot influence the next state until *two* rising clock edges after the change, as shown in Figure 5.16(b). The one-procedure description thus introduces some delay into the system's behavior.

Introducing such delay is not necessarily a bad thing. In many systems, the extra cycle delay may represent an insignificant change. For example, in Figure 5.16, both waveforms ultimately represent acceptable behavior of the three-cycles-high laser timer system—the output stays high for exactly three clock cycles after a button press. For that system, it is not important if the three cycles are shifted in time by one cycle; what's important is that the output stays high for exactly three cycles. The insignificance of delays in detecting input changes is further illustrated by the fact that external inputs are typically fed through a series of flip-flops in order to isolate circuits from flip-flop metastability issues—that series of flip-flops introduces several cycles of delay itself.

Therefore, a one-procedure synchronous description is actually a reasonable and popular approach for describing a HLSM during RTL design. If the extra cycle for reading inputs does not pose a timing problem, the one-procedure description yields simpler and easier-to-read descriptions.

The same two-procedure versus one-procedure discussion applies as equally to FSMs as it does to HLSMs. Specifically, an FSM can be described using one procedure. The most common one-procedure FSM description approach uses the same structure as the procedure in Figure 5.15, having only the state register and no additional registers. The procedure uses a single variable for the state register, a procedure sensitive to the clock input, and a single *if-else* statement containing a reset part and an actions/transitions case statement part.

5.4 IMPROVING TIMING REALISM

[SIMUL] DELAY CONTROL ON RIGHT SIDE OF ASSIGNMENT STATEMENTS

Real components do not compute their outputs instantly after the components' inputs change. Instead, real components have delay—after inputs change, the correct outputs do not appear until some time later. For example, suppose the comparator in the datapath of Figure 5.9 has a delay of 7 ns. In order to obtain a more accurate RTL simulation of the controller and datapath in that figure, a description could be extended to include such delays. Figure 5.17 shows how the description of Figure 5.11 could be extended to include a 7 ns delay for the comparator component, by using delay control.

Delay control was introduced in Chapter 2 for delaying the execution of a statement, achieved by prepending the delay control to a statement, as in the statement: "*#10 Y <= 0;*". However, delay control can also be inserted on the right side of an assignment statement, such as: "*Y <= #10 0;*". The prepended form delays execution of the statement that follows by 10 time units. In contrast, in the right side form, the statement is not delayed but instead executes immediately. Upon executing, however, the update of *Y* will be scheduled to occur 10 time units in the future.

In Figure 5.17, the assignment to *Cnt_Eq_0*, which models the datapath's comparator, have been extended with delay control indicating a 7 ns delay. To more fully model the datapath component delays, delay controls would also be added to the two *CntNext* assignments, modeling the delay of the mux and the decrementer.

```
`timescale 1 ns/1 ns

module LaserTimer(B, X, Clk, Rst);
...
   // DP CombLogic
   always @(Cnt_Sel, Cnt) begin
      if (Cnt_Sel==1)
         CntNext <= 2;
      else
         CntNext <= Cnt - 1;

      Cnt_Eq_0 <= #7 (Cnt==0)?1:0;
   end
...
```

Figure 5.17 Including a component's delay in a description.

Delays might be estimated from components existing in the component library that will be used in an implementation. Such delays are quite commonly included for low-level components like gates, muxes, registers, and so on. Including such delays in a description results in better timing accuracy during simulation, and can even detect timing problems. For example, if the clock period were shorter than the longest register-to-register delay in the datapath, the designer would notice that the datapath with delays computes incorrect results during simulation.

A tool synthesizing a circuit from a description having delays, like the description in Figure 5.17, would simply ignore the delay controls. Those controls serve to reflect the predicted timing behavior of the eventual implementation, and do *not* serve to guide the synthesis tool in creating that implementation.

Figure 5.18 illustrates the effect of including delays in a description. Figure 5.18(a) shows the simulation waveforms for the system when the comparator does not have any delay. That figure shows several internal variables, *Cnt*, *Cnt_Eq_0* (the comparator output), and *State*. Figure 5.18(b) shows the simulation waveforms for the description having the 7 ns comparator delay. Notice that the comparator's output, *Cnt_Eq_0*, is slightly shifted to the right, due to the delay.

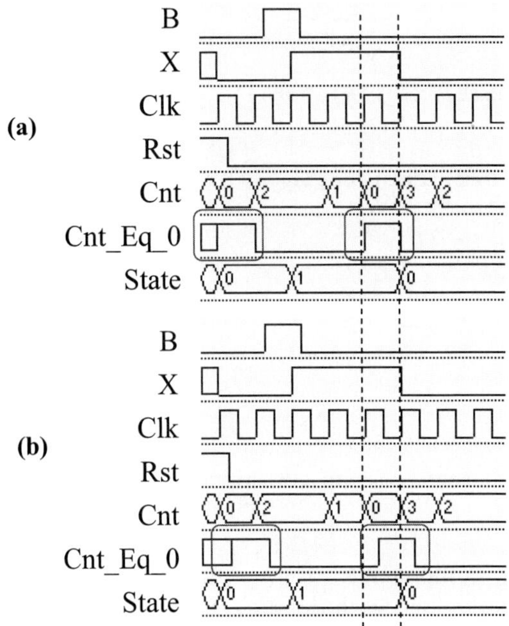

Figure 5.18 Simulation results: (a) without comparator delay, (b) with 7 ns delay.

5.5 ALGORITHMIC-LEVEL BEHAVIOR

In the early stages of design, a designer may want to describe a system's behavior at an even higher level of abstraction than the register-transfer level. Sometimes, the behavior is naturally first described as an algorithm. For example, consider a system that computes the sum of absolute differences (SAD) of the corresponding elements of two 256-element arrays. Such a computation is useful, for example, in video compression to determine the difference between two video frames. A SAD system block diagram appears in Figure 5.19(a). The system's algorithmic-level behavior is shown in Figure 5.19(b). The algorithm, which is written in pseudo-code and not in any particular language, indicates that the system is activated when the input *Go* becomes *1*. The algorithm then generates array indices from 0 to 255, one at a time. For each index, the algorithm computes the absolute value of the difference of the two array elements for that index, and adds that value to a running sum variable. The algorithm then writes the final sum to the system's output. Notice how simple and clear an algorithm-level description can be. A designer may wish to verify the correctness of the algorithm, before proceeding to design the system at the RT level. Some tools (known as behavioral synthesis or high-level synthesis tools) have evolved to attempt to synthesize algorithmic-level

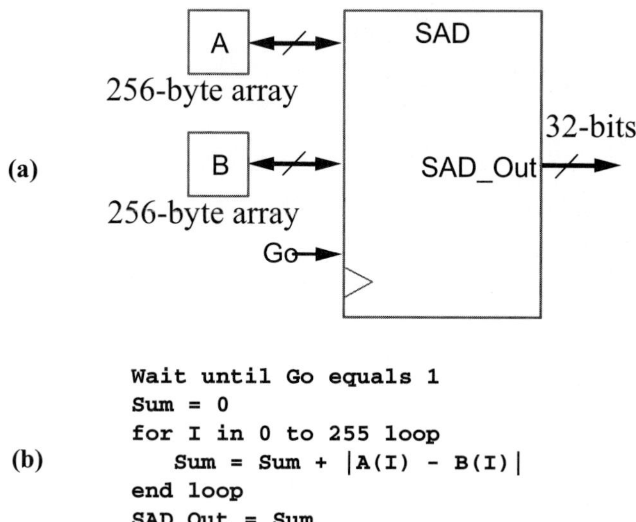
(a)
A
256-byte array
B
256-byte array
Go
SAD
SAD_Out
32-bits
(b)
Wait until Go equals 1
Sum = 0
for I in 0 to 255 loop
Sum = Sum + |A(I) - B(I)|
end loop
SAD_Out = Sum

Figure 5.19 Sum of absolute differences: (a) block diagram, (b) algorithm.

descriptions to circuits automatically, but most HDL users use algorithmic-level descriptions solely for early simulation purposes.

Figure 5.20 shows an algorithmic-level description of the SAD system's behavior. Although the two 256-element arrays *A* and *B* are external to the SAD system itself as shown in Figure 5.19(a), the algorithmic-level description initially declares those two arrays as part of the SAD module. Although not necessary, such declaration makes the initial description easier to create.

The description contains an always procedure having the main algorithm behavior. However, before that procedure, a user-defined function is declared. A ***user-defined function*** is typically intended to compute a value that will be used in an expression. The function defined in Figure 5.20 will be used to compute an absolute value, and is needed because Verilog does not contain a built-in absolute value operator. The first line, "*function integer ABS;*" defined the function's name to be *ABS*, and defines the function to return data of type integer. The second line, "*input integer IntVal;*", defines the function as having one input argument named *IntVal* of type integer. The contents of the function consist of a single statement. More procedural statements would be allowed in the function, as long as they didn't contain any time-controlling statements (delay control or event control) or any calls to tasks. The function's single statement assigns the return value of the function to be a positive version of the input argument. After the function *ABS* has been define, it can then be called by later parts of the description.

```
`timescale 1 ns/1 ns

module SAD(Go, SAD_Out);

   input Go;
   output reg [31:0] SAD_Out;

   reg [7:0] A [0:255];
   reg [7:0] B [0:255];
   integer Sum;
   integer I;

   function integer ABS;
      input integer IntVal;
      begin
         ABS = (IntVal>=0)?IntVal:-IntVal;
      end
   endfunction

   // Initialize Arrays
   initial $readmemh("MemA.txt", A);
   initial $readmemh("MemB.txt", B);

   always begin
      if (!(Go==1)) begin
         @(Go==1);
      end
      Sum = 0;
      for (I=0; I<=255; I=I+1) begin
         Sum = Sum + ABS(A[I] - B[I]);
      end
      #50;
      SAD_Out <= Sum;
   end
endmodule
```

Figure 5.20 Sum of absolute differences algorithmic-level description.

The description also declares memories *A* and *B* as 256-element arrays of bytes. Note that the description initializes those arrays using the built-in system task *$readmemh*. ***$readmemh*** is a system task intended to initialize memories by reading a file of hex numbers (with the file name being the function's first argument) and placing each number into successive elements of an array (with the array name being the second argument). The number of numbers in the file should match the number of elements in the array. The hex numbers in the file should not have a size or base format, and should be separated by white spaces, e.g., 00 FF A1 04 etc. Another system function, ***$readmemb***, instead reads a file of binary numbers (rather than hex numbers) into an array. Note that functions are called as the sole statement of an initial procedure. The syntax may look unusual; using a begin-end block may make the calls look more familiar:

```
initial begin
   $readmemh("MemA.txt", A);
end
```

The main procedure describing the algorithm is the always procedure at the bottom of Figure 5.20. The procedure's contents look very similar to the algorithm in Figure 5.19(b). The always procedure begins by waiting for *Go* to become *1*. It does so by checking if *Go* is already *1*, and if not, using the event control "*@(Go==1);*" Previous event controls involved a single event, such as "*@(X)*" or "*@(posedge Clk)*", or involved a list of events, such as "*@(X,Y)*". In Figure 5.20, however, the event control uses the expression "*@(Go==1)*". That event control does not merely detect a change in *Go*, but detects a change in *Go* such that *Go* becomes *1*. The word "change" is critical in the previous sentence. If *Go* is already *1* when the event control statement is reached during execution, the procedure still suspends at that event control. The procedure stays suspended at that statement until *Go* changes to *0* and then changes back to *1*. This behavior of an event control is somewhat counterintuitive, as many designers make the mistake of believing that if *Go* was *1* when reaching the statement, execution will simply proceed to the next statement without the procedure suspending. The description therefore uses an *if* statement to achieve the desired behavior of the procedure proceeding to compute the SAD if *Go* is already *1*.

The delay control "#50;" at the end of the procedure creates some delay (albeit a rather short one) between the time that Go becomes 1 and the time that the computed SAD value appears at the output. Including a delay at the end of the procedure also prevents an infinite simulation loop in which the procedure repeatedly executes without ever suspending if Go were always kept at 1.

Figure 5.21 provides a simple test vector procedure for the algorithm-level SAD description. The procedure pulses *Go_s*, waits for some time, and then checks that the computed SAD equals 4 (we happened to define the memory contents such that exactly four elements differed in A and B by one each). Simulation waveforms are shown in Figure 5.22. Note that the SAD output is initially unknown, due to the output not having been explicitly set to some value when the SAD procedure first executed. A better description would set the output to some value, likely during a reset.

```
`timescale 1 ns/1 ns

module Testbench();

   reg Go_s;
   wire [31:0] SAD_Out_s;

   SAD CompToTest(Go_s, SAD_Out_s);

   // Vector Procedure
   initial begin
      Go_s <= 0;
      #10 Go_s <= 1;
      #10 Go_s <= 0;
      #60 if (SAD_Out_s != 4) begin
         $display("SAD failed -- should equal 4");
      end
   end
endmodule
```

Figure 5.21 Simple testbench vector procedure for the SAD algorithmic-level description.

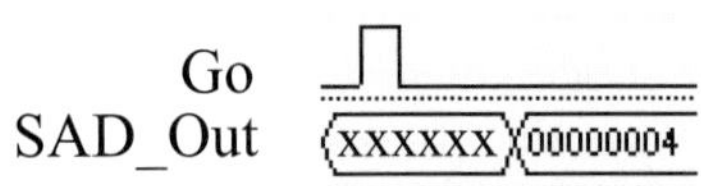

Figure 5.22 Waveforms for the SAD algorithmic-level description.

5.6 TOP-DOWN DESIGN—CONVERTING ALGORITHMIC-LEVEL BEHAVIOR TO RTL

Once satisfied that an algorithm is correct, a designer may wish to proceed to convert the algorithm-level behavior to an RTL description, as a means of moving towards an implementation of the system. The algorithm of Figure 5.20 can be recaptured as the HLSM shown in Figure 5.23. The HLSM can then be described as shown in Figure 5.24.

The HLSM can be tested using a testbench similar to that in Figure 5.21, except that the testbench should wait longer than just 60 ns for the SAD output to appear. By counting the number of HLSM states that must be visited to compute the SAD, one can determine a waiting time of (256*2+3) * (20 ns), where 20 ns is the clock period. Figure 5.25 shows a simple testbench for the HLSM.

Figure 5.26 provides the waveforms resulting from simulating the testbench, showing several internal variables to better demonstrate the HLSM's behavior during simulation.

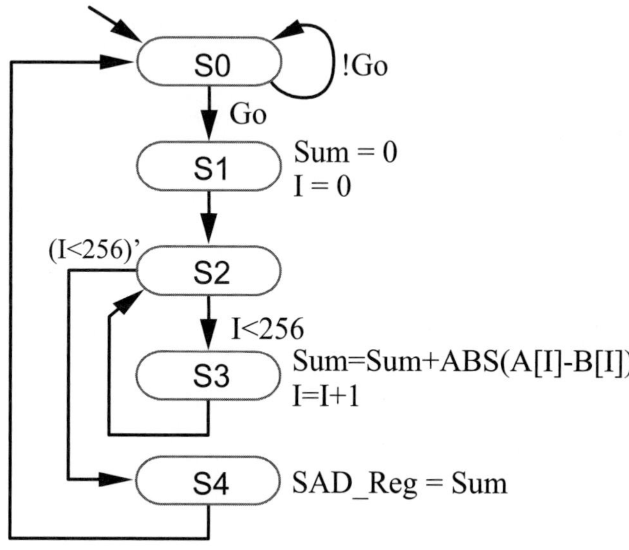

Figure 5.23 HLSM for the SAD system.

```
`timescale 1 ns/1 ns

module SAD(Go, SAD_Out, Clk, Rst);

   input Go;
   output [31:0] SAD_Out;
   input Clk, Rst;

   parameter S0 = 0, S1 = 1,
             S2 = 2, S3 = 3,
             S4 = 4;

   reg [7:0] A [0:255];
   reg [7:0] B [0:255];
   reg [2:0] State;
   integer Sum, SAD_Reg;
   integer I;

   function integer ABS;
      input integer IntVal;
      begin
         ABS = (IntVal>=0)?IntVal:-IntVal;
      end
   endfunction

   // Initialize Arrays
   initial $readmemh("MemA.txt", A);
   initial $readmemh("MemB.txt", B);

   // High-level state machine
   always @(posedge Clk) begin
      if (Rst==1) begin
         State <= S0;
         Sum <= 0;
         SAD_Reg <= 0;
         I <= 0;
      end
      else begin
         case (State)
            S0: begin
               if (Go==1)
                  State <= S1;
               else
                  State <= S0;
            end
            S1: begin
               Sum <= 0;
               I <= 0;
               State <= S2;
            end
            S2: begin
               if (!(I==255))
                  State <= S3;
               else
                  State <= S4;
            end
            S3: begin
               Sum <= Sum + ABS(A[I]-B[I]);
               I <= I + 1;
               State <= S2;
            end
            S4: begin
               SAD_Reg <= Sum;
               State <= S0;
            end
         endcase
      end
   end
endmodule
```

Figure 5.24 Description of the HLSM for the SAD system.

```
`timescale 1 ns/1 ns

module Testbench();

   reg Go_s;
   reg Clk_s, Rst_s;
   wire [31:0] SAD_Out_s;

   SAD CompToTest(Go_s, SAD_Out_s, Clk_s, Rst_s);

   // Clock Procedure
   always begin
      Clk_s <= 0;
      #10;
      Clk_s <= 1;
      #10;
   end   // Note: Procedure repeats

   // Vector Procedure
   initial begin
      Rst_s <= 1;
      Go_s <= 0;
      @(posedge Clk_s);
      Rst_s <= 0;
      Go_s <= 1;
      @(posedge Clk_s);
      Go_s <= 0;
      #((256*2+3)*20) if (SAD_Out_s != 4) begin
         $display("SAD failed -- should equal 4");
      end
   end
endmodule
```

Figure 5.25 Simple testbench vector procedure for the SAD HLSM description.

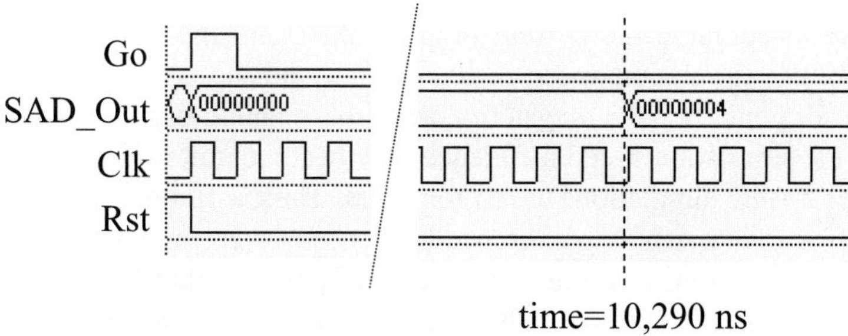

Figure 5.26 Waveforms for HLSM of the SAD system.

[SYNTH] AUTOMATED SYNTHESIS FROM THE ALGORITHMIC-LEVEL

Several commercial tools, known as ***behavioral synthesis*** or ***high-level synthesis*** tools, have been introduced in the 1990s and 2000s intending to automatically synthesize algorithmic-code to RTL code or even directly to circuits. Such tools have not yet been adopted as widely as RTL synthesis tools. Each tool imposes strong requirements and restrictions on the algorithmic-level code that may be synthesized, and those requirements and restrictions vary tremendously across tools. The quality of RTL code or circuits created from such tools also varies tremendously. Nevertheless, behavioral synthesis tools represent an interesting direction and may prove increasingly useful in coming years.

[SIMUL] SIMULATION SPEED

Higher-level descriptions not only have the advantage of requiring less time to create them and thus of being more suitable for initial system behavior definition, but also have the advantage of faster simulation. For example, the algorithmic-level description of the sum of absolute differences system may simulate faster than an HLSM description of that system, which in turn may simulate faster than a lower-level description like a gate-level description. When the system's *Go* input becomes *1*, the algorithmic-level description resumes a procedure that then executes a *for* loop that involves only a few thousand calculations in total to compute the output result. In contrast, the HLSM description would require tens of thousands of calculations by the simulator, which must suspend and resume the HLSM procedure nearly one thousand times in order to simulate the clock-controlled state machine of that procedure, performing dozens of calculations each time the procedure resumes in order to compute the current output values and the next state. For a small testbench, the simulation speed difference may not be noticeable. However, for a large testbench, or for a system comprised of hundreds or thousands of sub-systems, the simulation speed difference may become quite significant. It is not unusual for system simulations to run for hours. Thus, a 10 times difference in simulation speed may mean the difference between a 10-20 minute simulation versus a 2-3 hour simulation; a 100 times slower simulation could take days. Thus, high-level descriptions are favored early in the design process, when system behavior is being defined and refined. Low-level descriptions are necessary to achieve an implementation. High-level descriptions are also useful when integrating components in a large system, to see if those components interact properly from a behavioral perspective—the fast simulation speed allows for testing of a large variety of component interaction scenarios. Lower-level descriptions would be more suitable to verify detailed timing correctness of such large systems, but their slower simulation speed allows for only relatively few scenarios to be examined. For example, a system consisting of several microprocessor components described at a high level might be able to simulate minutes of microprocessor execution in a few hours, but might only be able to simulate a few seconds of microprocessor execution if described at a low level.

We previously showed how state machines could be modeled using two procedures where one procedure was combinational, or using one procedure where that procedure was sensitive only to a clock input. The latter will simulate much faster than the former, due to fewer procedure resumes and suspends. The difference may not be noticeable for small systems, but if a system contains hundreds or thousands of state machines, the difference can become quite significant.

5.7 MEMORY

Desired storage may initially be described merely using variables declared within a system's module, as was done in the SAD example of the previous section and as illustrated in Figure 5.27(a). However, refining the description towards an implementation may mean creating a description with that storage described as a separate memory component, as in Figure 5.27(b).

Describing memory separately begins by creating a new module representing a memory. A description for a simple read-only memory (ROM) appears in Figure 5.28. The memory description has an input port for the address, and an output port for the data. In this case, the bitwidth of those ports are the same, but they obviously can be different depending on the memory size and width. The description declares an array named *Memory* to store the memory's contents. The description uses a continuous assignment statement to always output the *Memory* data element corresponding to the current address input value.

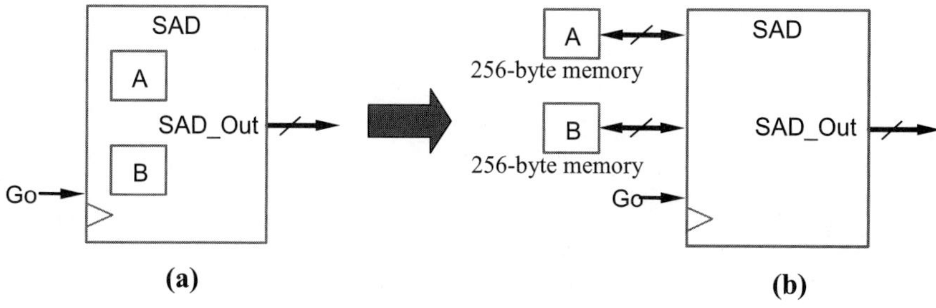

Figure 5.27 A more accurate system description may create memory as a separate component.

```
`timescale 1 ns/1 ns

module SADMem(Addr, Data);

   input [7:0] Addr;
   output [7:0] Data;

   reg [7:0] Memory [0:255];

   assign Data = Memory[Addr];
endmodule
```

Figure 5.28 Description of a simple read-only memory.

Figure 5.29 shows the HLSM for the SAD example, modified to access the external memory components. Rather than simply access *A* and *B* values, the HLSM must now set its address outputs *A_Addr* and *B_Addr*, and then use the returned data inputs *A_Data* and *B_Data*. Furthermore, because the HLSM is fully synchronous due to modeling it using a single procedure sensitive only to the clock input, the HLSM requires an extra state, *S3a*. Although the *A* and *B* memories will be combinational components, the extra state is necessary because the *A_Data* and *B_Data* inputs will only be sampled on clock edges due to the fully synchronous HLSM model being used.

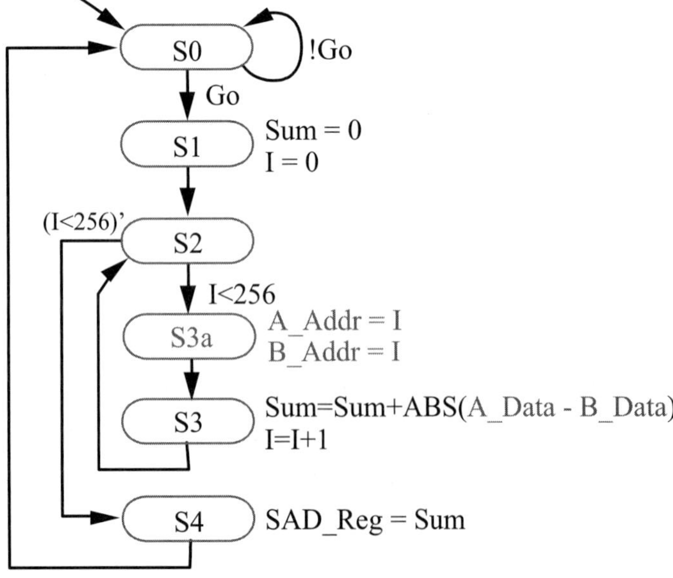

Figure 5.29 SAD HLSM modified to access the external memory components.

```
`timescale 1 ns/1 ns

module SAD(Go, A_Addr, A_Data,
           B_Addr, B_Data,
           SAD_Out, Clk, Rst);

   input Go;
   input [7:0] A_Data, B_Data;
   output reg [7:0] A_Addr, B_Addr;
   output [31:0] SAD_Out;
   input Clk, Rst;

   parameter S0 = 0, S1 = 1,
             S2 = 2, S3 = 3, S3a = 4,
             S4 = 5;

   reg [2:0] State;
   reg [31:0] Sum, SAD_Reg;
   integer I;

   function [7:0] ABSDiff;
      input [7:0] A;
      input [7:0] B;
      begin
         if (A>B) ABSDiff = A - B;
         else ABSDiff = B - A;
      end
   endfunction
```

Figure 5.30 SAD HLSM description with separate memory (part 1).

Figure 5.30 shows the first part of a description of the new SAD HLSM that uses memory components. The module declaration now includes the ports for interfacing with the external memory components. Furthermore, the description now defines a function *ABSDiff* that computes the absolute value of the difference of two vectors.

Figure 5.31 shows the second part of the new HLSM description. The part shown illustrates the new state *S3a*, corresponding to the HLSM of Figure 5.29. Notice how the accesses to items *A* and *B* are now completely through address and data ports. Also notice that state *S3* now calls function *ABSDiff* rather than *ABS*. A synthesis tool would replace that function call by the contents of the function itself. In other words, the description could have included *ABSDiff*'s *if-else* statement directly in state *S3*. However, using the function leads to improved readability of the HLSM. (We point out that we violated our own guideline of always using a begin-end block for an *if* statement. We did so merely so that the code figure would fit in this textbook).

```
    always @(posedge Clk) begin
        if (Rst==1) begin
            A_Addr <= 0;
            B_Addr <= 0;
            State <= S0;
            Sum <= 0;
            SAD_Reg <= 0;
            I <= 0;
        end
        else begin
            case (State)
                S0: begin
                    if (Go==1)
                        State <= S1;
                    else
                        State <= S0;
                end
                S1: begin
                    Sum <= 0;
                    I <= 0;
                    State <= S2;
                end
                S2: begin
                    if (!(I==255))
                        State <= S3a;
                    else
                        State <= S4;
                end
                S3a: begin
                    A_Addr <= I;
                    B_Addr <= I;
                    State <= S3;
                end
                S3: begin
                    Sum <= Sum +
                     ABSDiff(A_Data, B_Data);
                    I <= I + 1;
                    State <= S2;
                end
                S4: begin
                    SAD_Reg <= Sum;
                    State <= S0;
                end
            endcase
        end
    end

    assign SAD_Out = SAD_Reg;

endmodule
```

Figure 5.31 SAD HLSM description with separate memory (part 2).

```
module Testbench();
   reg Go_s;
   wire [7:0] A_Addr_s, B_Addr_s;
   wire [7:0] A_Data_s, B_Data_s;
   reg Clk_s, Rst_s;
   wire [31:0] SAD_Out_s;

   parameter ClkPeriod = 20;

   SAD CompToTest(Go_s, A_Addr_s, A_Data_s,
                  B_Addr_s, B_Data_s,
                  SAD_Out_s, Clk_s, Rst_s);
   SADMem SADMemA(A_Addr_s, A_Data_s);
   SADMem SADMemB(B_Addr_s, B_Data_s);

   // Clock Procedure
   always begin
      Clk_s <= 0; #(ClkPeriod/2);
      Clk_s <= 1; #(ClkPeriod/2);
   end

   // Initialize Arrays
   initial $readmemh("MemA.txt", SADMemA.Memory);
   initial $readmemh("MemB.txt", SADMemB.Memory);

   // Vector Procedure
   initial begin
      ... // Reset behavior not shown
      Go_s <= 1;
      @(posedge Clk_s);
      Go_s <= 0;
      #((256*3+3)*ClkPeriod) if (SAD_Out_s != 4) begin
         $display("SAD failed -- should equal 4");
      end
   end
endmodule
```

Figure 5.32 SAD HLSM testbench with memory components.

Figure 5.32 shows a testbench for the SAD system with separate memory instances. The testbench declares the variables and nets needed for connecting module instances together, and then instantiates and connects the instances. Note that a testbench can instantiate multiple modules for testing, rather than instantiating just one module. To the extent possible, designers should always also test modules separately, before testing them together in a single testbench.

The testbench then defines the clock, memory initialization, and vector procedures. The memory initialization procedures again use the *$readmemh* function to initialize arrays within the *SADMemA* and *SADMemB* memories by specifying the arrays to initialized as *SADMemA.Memory* and *SADMemB.Memory*. The vector procedure is similar to the procedure of the previous SAD HLSM without external

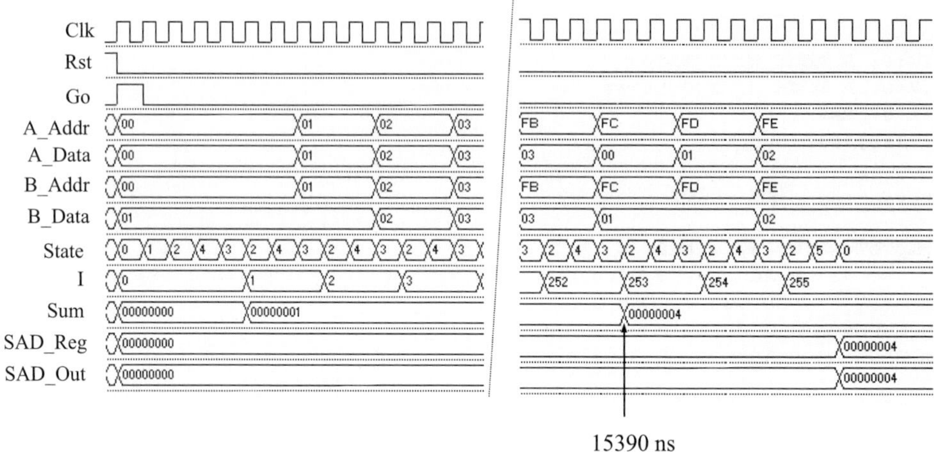

Figure 5.33 Waveforms for SAD HLSM with memory components.

memory components, except that the procedure must wait longer for the SAD output to appear, due to the extra state in the HLSM. Thus, rather than waiting (256*2+3) * (20 ns), the procedure waits (256*3+3) * (20 ns).

The testbench in Figure 5.32 has also been improved by declaring a parameter named *ClkPeriod* to represent the clock's period of 20 ns, and using that parameter in the clock and vector procedures, rather than hardcoding the 20 ns value throughout. Declaring such a parameter enables a designer to easily change the clock period just by changing one number, rather than having to change multiple numbers scattered throughout the code (and possibly forgetting to change the number in one place or changing a number when it should not have been changed).

Finally, Figure 5.33 shows waveforms generated from the testbench. Waveforms for the address and data signals now appear. The final SAD output also appears, although it appears later than in Figure 5.26, due to the extra state in the HLSM. Generally, converting a design from higher-levels to levels closer to an implementation yield increasing timing accuracy.

CHAPTER 6

Verilog Mini-Reference

6.1 BASIC SYNTAX

COMMENTS

Comments can be used to provide annotations about Verilog code to provide designers with additional information regarding the code. Verilog comments do not affect the simulation or synthesis of a Verilog description, but are very useful to human readers. Verilog ***comments*** can be either single line comments or block comments. A ***single line comment*** begins with the two forward slashes, "//", and continues until the end of the line. Single line comments may start on the same line following a Verilog statement. However, a statement cannot start on the same line following a single line comment, as the statement would be considered part of the comment. A ***block comment*** begins with "/*", and continues until the end of the comment indicated by the characters "*/". Block comments may span multiple lines and begin or end on lines containing valid Verilog statements. Verilog does not support nested block comments, and the appearance of "//" within a block comment is ignored.

Examples:

```
// Example of a single line comment
A <= 0; // Reset condition

/* Comments that span multiple lines
can be specified using a block comment */
```

```
/* The following statement is valid */ B <= 0;

A <= 0; /* Reset condition */
```

IDENTIFIERS

User-defined names are ***identifiers*** used within Verilog to describe parts of a design. User-defined names, or identifiers, must start with a letter or underscore ("_"), optionally followed by any sequence of letters, digits, underscores, or dollar signs ("*$*"). Verilog is ***case sensitive***, meaning there is a difference between upper and lower-case letters.

Examples of valid identifiers:

```
A
B14
Wire_23
test_module
Test_module // different from test_module
_Go_$_$
```

Examples of invalid identifiers:

```
input    // keyword
4x1Mux   // does not begin with letter or underscore
$in4     // does not begin with letter or underscore
```

KEYWORDS

A ***keyword***, also referred to as a ***reserved word***, is an identifier that has special significance in the language and may not be used as a user-defined name within a Verilog description. The full list of Verilog keywords is presented here. Note that Verilog is case sensitive and all keywords are lower-case.

```
always          and             assign
automatic       begin           buf
bufif0          bufif1          case
casex           casez           cell
cmos            config          deassign
default         defparam        design
disable         edge            else
end             endcase         endconfig
endfunction     endgenerate     endmodule
endprimitive    endspecify      endtable
```

```
endtask          event              for
force            forever            fork
function         generate           genvar
highz0           highz1             if
ifnone           incdir             include
initial          inout              input
instance         integer            join
large            liblist            library
localparam       macromodule        medium
module           nand               negedge
nmos             nor                noshowcancelled
not              notif0             notif1
or               output             parameter
pmos             posedge            primitive
pull0            pull1              pulldown
pullup           pulsestyle_onevent pulsestyle_ondetect
rcmos            real               realtime
reg              release            repeat
rnmos            rpmos              rtran
rtranif0         rtranif1           scalared
showcancelled    signed             small
specify          specparam          strong0
strong1          supply0            supply1
table            task               time
tran             tranif0            tranif1
tri              tri0               tri1
triand           trior              trireg
unsigned         use                uwire
vectored         wait               wand
weak0            weak1              while
wire             wor                xnor
xor
```

NUMBERS

A ***number*** is the representation of a numeric value. Numbers are used to assign specific values to variables, parameters, and similar items, and within expressions that include a specific value.

Integer Constant

An ***integer constant*** number is an integer value specified in one of four bases: decimal, hexadecimal, octal, or binary. Integer constants can be specified as a simple decimal number or as a based constant. A simple decimal number is decimal values specified as sequence of decimal digits. Simple decimal numbers are considered signed integer numbers but may be preceded by the "+" or "-" unary sign operators to specify the value's sign. All negative numbers are represented using twos-complement form. An integer constant can include any number of underscores to separate digits within the number, with the restriction that a number cannot begin with an underscore. Underscores have no effect on the value of the number but may improve the readability.

Examples:

```
123
45
-45
1_450_891
```

A ***based constant number*** is an integer number specified as three parts: the size of the value, an apostrophe followed by the base indicator, and the sequence of digits representing the desired integer value. The size part is optional and specifies the size of the integer constant in bits. The base indicator specifies the base of the number as a single *case insensitive* letter, namely *d* or *D* for decimal, *h* or *H* for hexadecimal, *o* or *O* for octal, and *b* or *B* for binary. The base indicator may be followed by an optional sign indicator, *s* or *S*, indicating the value to be specified is a signed number. The sign indicator does not change the value of the specified number, but rather how that number should be interpreted. A based constant specified without the sign indicator is considered an unsigned value. A based constant may also be preceded by the '+' or '-' unary operators to specify the value's sign, but care should be taken when combined with a signed based constant. A based constant can include any number of underscores to separate digits within the number, with the restriction that a number cannot begin with an underscore. Underscores have no effect on the value of the number but may improve the readability.

Examples:

```
32
'b1     // equivalent to decimal value 1
4'b1101
8'd255 // equivalent to 8-bit decimal value 255
8'hB5   // equivalent to 8'HB5, 8'Hb5, and 8'hb5
4'hsF   // equivalent to decimal value -1
-4'h1   // equivalent to decimal value -1

// The following examples all represent the
// the same value

12'b111111111111
12'b1111_1111_1111
12'o7777
12'hFFF
```

Real Constant

A ***real constant*** number defines a real value represented as an IEEE standard double-precision floating point number. Real numbers may be defined using either decimal or scientific notation. A real number specified using a decimal point must include at least one digit on both sides of the decimal point. A real constant can include any number of underscores to separate digits within either notation, with the restriction that a number cannot begin with an underscore. Underscores have no effect on the value of the number but may improve the readability.

Examples:

```
3.14159
0.5
2e-5
1.25e10
1_.2_5e1_0   // equivalent to 1.25e10
```

Examples of invalid real constants:

```
.25     // No digit on left side of decimal point
1.E3    // No digit on right side of decimal point
```

STRINGS

A ***string*** is a sequence of characters enclosed between two quotation marks. If a quotation mark needs to be part of the string literal itself, a backward slash followed by a quotation mark, " \" ", within the string can be used to represent the quotation mark itself. A string must fit on a single line. The concatenation operator, "*{}*", can be used to concatenate multiple strings on separate lines together. If a string is used as an operand within an expression or assignment statement, the string will be treated as an unsigned integer constant corresponding to the concatenation of the 8-bit ASCII values for each character within the string.

Examples:

```
"Error: File not found."

{"This string is very long and looks better ",
 "when split into multiple strings on separate " ,
 "lines concatenated together"}

"\"Hi\"" // A string containing quotation marks
```

6.2 DECLARATIONS

NET (WIRE)

```
wire Name1, Name2, Name3;
```

A ***net*** is a data type that does not store a value, but rather is used for connections, and derives its value from what it is connected to. A net declaration must define the net type and net name. A net may be declared as ***wire***, ***supply0***, ***supply1***, ***tri***, ***triand***, ***trior***, ***tri0***, ***tri1***, ***uwire***, ***wand***, or ***wor***, although we only consider ***wire*** nets in this book, which represent bits. A wire net declaration defines a single bit net that may be connected to a module's inputs or outputs within a ***module instantiation***, or may be assigned a value within a ***continuous assignment statement***. A multi-bit vector of wire nets may also be declared using a ***range specification*** and defines a collection of nets, which is often more convenient than declaring each bit separately. Multiple nets of the same type can be declared within a single net declaration statement, where each net name is separated by a comma.

Examples:

```
wire B, X, F;
wire [3:0] A_s; // A multi-bit vector of wire nets
```

MODULE

```
module (Ports);
   Port_Declarations

   Module_Statements
endmodule;
```

A ***module*** definition defines an module's *interface* to the outside world, including the module's name, inputs, and outputs. A module definition also includes the declaration of the module's ports.

Ports

```
input Port1, Port2, Port3;
output Port1, Port2, Port3;
output reg Port1, Port2, Port3;
```

The module's inputs and outputs, known as ***ports,*** appear in a list contained between the parentheses just after the module's name. Each port must then appear in an ***input***, ***output***, or ***inout*** declaration to indicate the port's direction. Multiple ports of the same type may be declared within a single port declaration, where each port name is separated by a comma. By default, all outputs are assumed to be ***wire*** nets. An output port may also be declared as ***reg*** variable data type either within a separate ***reg*** variable declaration or within a single ***output reg*** declaration.

Example:

```
module And2(X, Y, F);

   input X, Y;
   output F;
   reg F;

   // Module's statements
endmodule

module And2(X, Y, F);

   input X, Y;
   output reg F;

   // Module's statements
endmodule
```

PARAMETER

```
parameter Name1 = Value1, Name2 = Value2;
parameter Name = Constant_Expression;
```

A ***parameter*** is a constant value defined within a module and represents a fixed value that cannot be changed within the module's definition. A ***parameter declaration*** statement must specify the parameter name and define the value for the parameter. Multiple parameters of the same type can be declared within a single parameter declaration statement, where each parameter and value assignment are separated by commas. While the value of a parameter cannot be modified within the module's definition, the parameter's value can be modified within a module instantiation's parameter assignment or by a ***defparam*** statement and can vary across multiple instances of the modules. A parameter may be assigned a constant expression involving other parameters. Parameters used within the specification of an input or output port must be declared before the port declaration. For example, a vector output port *S* may be declared as "*output [Width-1:0] S;*" where *Width* is parameter declared before the port declaration. If *Width* is initialized with the value 32, the output port declaration for *S* is equivalent to "*output [31:0] S;*".

Examples:

```
parameter S_Off = 0, S_On1 = 1;
parameter ClkPeriod = 20;
parameter Rows = 10, Cols = 2;
parameter Size = Rows * Cols;
parameter [2:0] C6 = 3'b110;

// Module definition with parameter Width
module Add4(A, B, S);

   parameter Width = 32;
   input [Width-1:0] A, B;
   output [Width-1:0] S;
   reg [Width-1:0] S;

   always @(A, B) begin
      S <= A + B;
   end
endmodule
```

Local Parameter

```
localparam Name1 = Value1, Name2 = Value2;
localparam Name = Constant_Expression;
```

A ***local parameter*** is a constant value defined within a module that represents a fixed value that cannot be changed within the module's definition. A ***local parameter declaration*** statement starts with the keyword ***localparam*** and must specify the parameter name and define the value for the parameter. Multiple parameters of the same type can be declared within a single local parameter declaration statement, where each parameter and value assignment are separated by a comma. Unlike parameters, local parameters cannot be modified within a module instantiation's parameter assignment or by a ***defparam*** statement, but can still be assigned constant expressions involving other parameters and local parameters.

Example:

```
localparam S_Off = 0, S_On1 = 1;
```

```
localparam ClkPeriod = 20;
localparam C15 = 3'hF;
```

VARIABLE (REG)

```
reg Name1, Name2, Name3;
reg Name = Value;
```

A ***variable*** data type holds its values between assignments. A variable declaration statement must define the variable type and variable name and can optionally define an initial value for the variable. Note that assigning an initial value to a variable is generally not synthesizable, but it can be useful for testbenches and simulation. A variable may be declared as ***reg***, ***integer***, ***real***, ***time***, or ***realtime***, although we only consider the *reg* kind. A reg variable data type is a 1-bit variable that can be assigned a value within a procedure, although a multi-bit vector of type reg may be declared using a ***range specification***. A range specification defines the vector's most significant bit position, least significant bit position, ordering of the bits within the vector, as well as implicitly defining the number of bits within the vector. Variables of type reg may be connected to a module's inputs within a module instantiation, but may not be connected to a module's outputs. Multiple variables of the same type can be declared within a single variable declaration statement, where each variable name is separated by a comma.

Examples:

```
reg A;
reg [1:0] IReg = 2'b11;
reg X_s, Y_s, F_s;
```

6.3 STATEMENTS

ASSIGNMENT STATEMENT

Blocking Assignment

```
Variable_Name = Expression;
```

A ***blocking assignment statement*** is a procedural assignment using the "=" operator to assign a value to a variable. A blocking assignment *updates* the left-side variable with the value of the right-side expression *before proceeding* to execute the next statement.

Examples:

```
Sum = 0;
S5 = A5 + B5 + Ci;
```

Non-blocking Assignment

```
Variable_Name <= Expression;
```

A ***non-blocking assignment statement*** is a procedural assignment statement using the "<=" operator to assign a value to a variable. A blocking assignment statement *schedules an update* of the left-side variable with the value of the right-side expression *and proceeds* to execute the next statement. The variable's value will be will be updated at the end of the current simulation cycle.

Examples:

```
F <= X & Y;
Q <= 4'b0001;
I_reg <= I_reg + 1;
```

Continuous Assignment

```
assign Net_Name = Expression;
```

A ***continuous assignment statement*** is an assignment statement starting with the keyword ***assign*** that assigns to a net the specified right-size expression whenever the values used within the expression change. The continuous assignment statement describes combinational logic and is similar to an always procedure whose event control contains all nets or variables used within the right-side expression and contains a single assignment statement. However, a continuous assignment statement is used to assign a value to a net, not a variable.

Examples:

```
// Module with continuous assignment statement
module ShiftReg32(Q, Shr, Shr_in, Clk, Rst);

   output [31:0] Q;
   input Shr, Shr_in;
```

```
   input Clk, Rst;

   reg [31:0] R;
   integer Index;

   always @(posedge Clk) begin
      // Procedure statements
   end
   assign Q = R; // Continuous assignment
endmodule


// Procedure equivalent of the continuous assignment
// statement "assign Q = R;".
// Q must instead have been declared as reg
always @(R) begin
   Q <= R;
end
```

CASE STATEMENT

```
case (Expression)
   Case_Item:
      Case_Item_Statement
   Case_Item:
      Case_Item_Statement
   default:
      Case_Item_Statement
endcase

case (Expression)
   Case_Item: begin
      Case_Item_Statements
   end
   Case_Item: begin
      Case_Item_Statements
   end
   default: begin
      Case_Item_Statements
   end
endcase
```

A ***case statement*** selects for execution one statement among several possible statements, based on the value of the case statement's expression enclosed within parentheses following the keyword ***case***. The case statement will evaluate the case expression and execute the statement, or statements enclosed within a sequential (begin-end) block, for the ***case item*** whose expression value matches the value of the case statement's expression. The first case item (from top to bottom) whose expression matches the case statement's expression value will execute, causing remaining case items to be ignored. In the first example below, the expression is simply *State*. The possible values of *State* are the expressions *S_Off*, *S_On1*, *S_On2*, and *S_On3*, where each expression is part of a case item that includes an associated statement, which is commonly a begin-end block as in this example.

If no case item expression matches, then nothing executes. However, a well constructed case statement should define all possible alternatives and define a sequence of statements to execute for each case item. The last case item within a case statement may define a ***default*** case item whose statements will execute if none of the earlier case item expressions match.

Example:

```
case (State)
   S_Off: begin
      X <= 0;
      if (B == 0)
         StateNext <= S_Off;
      else
         StateNext <= S_On1;
   end
   S_On1: begin
      X <= 1;
      StateNext <= S_On2;
   end
   S_On2: begin
      X <= 1;
      StateNext <= S_On3;
   end
   S_On3: begin
      X <= 1;
      StateNext <= S_Off;
   end
endcase

// Case statement with default case item
case (Sel)
   2'b00:
      D <= I0;
   2'b01:
      D <= I1;
   2'b10:
      D <= I2;
```

```
    2'b11:
       D <= I3;
    default:
       D <= 'bz;
endcase
```

IF-ELSE STATEMENT

```
if (Expression) begin
   If_Statements
end

if (Expression) begin
   If_Statements
end
else begin
   Else_Statements
end

if (Expression) begin
   If_Statements
end
else if (Expression) begin
   Else_If_Statements
end
else begin
   Else_Statements
end
```

An ***if-else statement*** (also known as a ***conditional statement***) evaluates the expression defined within parentheses following the ***if*** keyword and executes the following statement, or statements enclosed within a sequential (begin-end) block, if the expression evaluates to true. An expression is said to evaluate to ***true*** if that expression evaluates to any non-zero value. If the expression evaluates to false, the *if* part's statements will be skipped and the statement, or statements, within the optional ***else*** part will be executed.

Often multiple possibilities, not just the two possibilities considered in an *if-else* statement, must be represented. Multiple possibilities can be described by stringing *if-else* statements together. Such a description is common enough to be known separately as an ***if-else-if*** construct, even though the construct is not actually a distinct language construct.

Good practice dictates using a begin-end block for the *if* and *else* parts even when those parts consist of a single statement, the exception being when forming an *if-else-if* construct.

Examples:

```
// if statement
if (Ld == 1) begin
   Q <= I;
end

// if-else statement
if (Cnt_Sel==1) begin
   CntNext <= 2;
end
else begin
   CntNext <= Cnt - 1;
end

// if-else-if statement
if ($signed({1'b0,A}) < B) begin
   Gt <= 0; Eq <= 0; Lt <= 1;
end
else if ($signed({1'b0,A}) > B) begin
   Gt <= 1; Eq <= 0; Lt <= 0;
end
else begin
   Gt <= 0; Eq <= 1; Lt <= 0;
end
```

LOOP STATEMENT

A ***loop statement*** defines a sequence of statements that will be executed repeatedly some number of times.

For Loop

```
for (Initialization; Condition; Update) begin
   Loop_Statements
end
```

A ***for loop statement*** is typically used to describe a loop whose statements execute a specific number of times, typically controlled by a ***index variable*** used in conjunction with the *for* loop statement to keep count of the number of *for* loop iterations. The *for* loop statement begins with the keyword ***for*** and consists of three parts, contained in parentheses and separated by semicolons. The first part is the *initialization* part, which is executed only once, at the start of the *for* loop's execution. The second part is the *condition* part, which is checked before each loop iteration. If the condition is true (non-zero), the loop executes its sub-statements. An expression is said to evaluate to ***true*** if that expression evaluates to any non-zero value. After the sub-statements execute once, the third part of the *for* loop statement, the *index variable update* part, executes. That part typically updates the index variable. For example, a *for* loop defined as "*for (Index=0; Index<=30; Index=Index+1) begin*" will execute a total of 31 times.

Although a *for* loop will execute the loop one iteration at a time, during synthesis a *for* loop will usually be expanded, or unrolled, such that all iterations of the loop will be executed simultaneously.

Example:

```
for (Index=0; Index<=30; Index=Index+1) begin
   R[Index] <= R[Index+1];
end
```

Repeat Loop

```
repeat (Expression) begin
   Loop_Statements
end
```

A ***repeat loop statement*** is a loop that executes its sub-statement a fixed number of times determined by the value of the expression specified within parentheses following the ***repeat*** keyword. The loop's sub-statement is typically a sequential (begin-end) block containing one or more statements. The *repeat* loop is similar to a *for* loop that iterates over a fixed range without the need for an index variable.

Example:

```
// Loop will wait for 10 rising clock edges
repeat (10) begin
   @(posedge Clk_s);
end
```

While Loop

```
while (Condition) begin
   Loop_Statements
end
```

A ***while loop statement*** is a loop that continues to execute its statements as long as the loop's condition evaluates to true (non-zero). An expression is said to evaluate to ***true*** if that expression evaluates to any non-zero value. If the loop's condition evaluates to true, the loop's sub-statement, or sub-statements, will be executed and the condition is checked again. If the loop condition evaluates to false, the loop's execution is complete. The loop's sub-statement is typically a sequential (begin-end) block containing one or more statements.

Example:

```
while ($feof(FileId) == 0) begin
   // File IO statements
end
```

For all of the above loop types, good practice dictates using a begin-end block for a loop's sub-statements, even when those sub-statements consist of only a single statement.

NULL

```
;
```

A ***null*** statement is a statement consisting of nothing but a semicolon.

PROCEDURE

A ***procedure*** is a sequence of statements executed by a simulator one at a time, starting from the first statement. Verilog supports four types of procedures, of which the ***always procedure*** and ***initial procedure*** and described here.

Always Procedure

```
always begin
   Procedure_Statements
end

always @* begin
   Procedure_Statements
end

always @(Event1, Event2, Event3) begin
   Procedure_Statements
end

always @(Event1 or Event2 or Event3) begin
   Procedure_Statements
end
```

An ***always procedure*** is a procedure that is executed at the start of simulation and then repeated, executing the statement or statements within the procedure repeatedly. *An always procedure thus describes an infinite loop.* An always procedure starts with the keyword ***always*** followed optionally by the procedure's *event control*.

The ***event control*** indicates that the procedure should only execute its statements when at least one of the listed events occurs. A change of value of a listed item is considered an ***event***. The list is often called a *sensitivity list*, and the procedure is said to be ***sensitive*** to the listed items. The event control begins with the "@" symbol followed by the list of events enclosed within parentheses, where the events are separated by commas, although Verilog also allows separation using the keyword ***or***. Events may also be declared as ***posedge*** and ***negedge***. A positive edge event, ***posedge,*** also known as a ***rising edge***, indicates an event defined by a transition from *0* to *1* (or *x* to *1*). A negative edge event, ***negedge***, also known as a ***falling edge***, indicates an event defined by a transition from *1* to *0* (or *x* to *0*).

The event control may be also listed as "**@***", known as an implicit event control expression (or *implicit sensitivity list*), which automatically adds all nets and variables that are read by the procedure's statements to the event control expression. "*@(*)*" is equivalent to "@*".

Failing to include any event control or delays in an always procedure results in an infinite simulation loop that prevents simulation from proceeding forward in simulated time, and is thus generally considered to be a coding error.

Examples:

```
// Always procedure with event control
always @(X, Y) begin
   F <= X & Y;
end

// Always procedure with posedge event in
// event control
always @(posedge Clk) begin
   if (Rst == 1)
      Q <= 4'b0000;
   else
      Q <= I;
end

// Always procedure without event control
// (but with delays instead)
always begin
   Clk_s <= 0;
   #10;
   Clk_s <= 1;
```

```
   #10;
end

// Always procedure with implicit event control
always @*
begin
   if (S1==0 && S0==0)
      D <= I0;
   else if (S1==0 && S0==1)
      D <= I1;
   else if (S1==1 && S0==0)
      D <= I2;
   else
      D <= I3;
end
```

Initial Procedure

```
initial begin
   Procedure_Statements
end
```

An ***initial procedure*** is a procedure that executes its statements at the start of simulation, but only executes once and never repeats.

Examples:

```
initial begin
   // Test all possible input combinations
   Y_s <= 0; X_s <= 0;
   #10 Y_s <= 0; X_s <= 1;
   #10 Y_s <= 1; X_s <= 0;
   #10 Y_s <= 1; X_s <= 1;
end

initial $readmemh("MemA.txt", SADMemA.Memory);
```

MODULE INSTANTIATION

```
Module_Type Instance_Name (Port_Connection);
Module_Type #(Parameter_Assignment) Instance_Name
   (Port_Connection);
```

A ***module instantiation*** statement creates a single instance of a module in a circuit, and describes how that instance connects with circuit wires. A module instantiation statement specifies a unique name for the module instance, the type of module being instantiated, a port connection, and an optional parameter assignment.

Port Connection

```
(Variable_Net1, Variable_Net2);
(.Port(Variable_Net1), .Port(Variable_Net2));
```

The ***port connections*** part of a module instantiation statement connects the module instance's ports to the variables and nets in the circuit. Variables and nets may be explicitly defined by reg and wire declarations, respectively. An ***ordered port connection*** is a list of variables and nets in parentheses separated by commas, where each variable or net in the list connects to a port of the module instance, according to the order of ports in the module instance's original module definition. A ***named port connection*** explicitly connects the module instance's ports by name to the variable or nets within the circuit. The named port connection is a list of named connections separated by commas, where each named connection begins with a period followed by the instance's port name with the variable or net connected to the port enclosed within parentheses.

Examples:

```
// Module instantiation with ordered port connection
Add4 CompToTest(A_s, B_s, S_s);

// Module instantiation with named port connection
Add4 CompToTest(.A(A_s), .S(S_s), .B(B_s));
```

Parameter Assignment

```
#(Value, Value);
```

The module instance ***parameter assignment*** associates values with module instance's parameters. The parameter assignment is part of a module instantiation and is specified between the module type and the instance name. A module instance parameter assignment starts with a "#" followed by an ordered list of values specified within parentheses and separated by commas, where each value in the list specifies the value for a parameter within the module instance, according to the order of parameter declarations in the module instance's original module definition. The parameter assignment does not need to specify values for all parameters defined within the module instance, but specific parameters' values cannot be skipped within the module instance parameter assignment and are strictly assigned in the order the parameters were declared. A parameter assignment overrides the value assigned to a parameter within a module definition itself. Local parameters cannot be assigned values with a module instance parameter assignment.

Example:

```
// Module with parameter Width
module Add4(A, B, S);

   parameter Width = 32;
   input [Width-1:0] A, B;
   output [Width-1:0] S;
   reg [Width-1:0] S;

   always @(A, B) begin
      S <= A + B;
   end
endmodule

// Module instantiation with parameter assignment
// Width will be 4, overriding the 32
Add4 #(4) CompToTest (A_s, B_s, S_s);
```

TIMING CONTROL

Delay Control

```
# Delay Statement;
Variable_Name <= # Delay Expression;
Variable_Name = # Delay Expression;
assign #Delay Net_Name = Expression;
```

A ***delay control*** tells the simulator to delay a statement's execution or a statement's assignment for the number of time units specified following the "#" symbol. A delay control preceding the left side of a statement will delay the execution of the statement for the specified number of time units.

A delay control can also be inserted on the right side of an assignment statement. In the right side form, the assignment statement is not delayed, but instead executes immediately and will schedule the variable's update to occur at the specified number of time units in the future. If the assignment is a blocking assignment statement, execution does not proceed to the next statement until the update occurs. If the assignment is a non-blocking assignment, execution proceeds without waiting for the update to occur.

Examples:

```
#10 A_s <= 4'b0011;
A_s <= #10 4'd5;
B_s = #5 4'd2;
assign #10 Q = R;
#5;
#((256*3+3)*ClkPeriod) if (SAD_Out_s != 4)
   $display("SAD failed -- should equal 4");
```

Event Control

```
@(Event) Statement;
@(Event1, Event2, Event3) Statement;
@(Event1 or Event2 or Event3) Statement;
```

An ***event control*** may precede a statement to synchronize that statement's execution with an event. The event control indicates that the statement, or statements defined within a sequential (begin-end) block, should only execute when at least one of the listed events occurs. Details of event control syntax appears in the earlier section on *always* procedures on page 145.

Examples:

```
@(posedge Clk_s);
@(Go==1);
```

Timescale Directive

```
`timescale Time_Unit/Time_Precision
```

A ***timescale directive*** indicates to the compiler (the program that converts the HDL file to input for a simulator) that from this point forward, 1 time unit corresponds to a particular unit of measurement of time. The grave accent character, "`", indicates that this is a directive to the compiler. Note that the grave accent character is different from an apostrophe or single quote, slanting from top-left to bottom-right. The first part of the directive defines the unit of time for delays. Valid time units are: ***s*** (seconds), ***ms*** (milliseconds), ***us*** (microseconds), ***ns*** (nanoseconds), ***ps*** (picoseconds), and ***fs*** (femtoseconds). The second part defines the precision used for internal time computations. Note that all times described above correspond to simulated time, not real time.

Examples:

```
`timescale 1 ns/1 ns
`timescale 1 ns/1 ps
```

Wait Statement

```
wait (Expression) Statement;
```

A ***wait statement*** is a special form of an ***event control*** that is level-sensitive. The wait statement will evaluate the expression specified within parentheses following the keyword ***wait***, and if the expression evaluates to true (non-zero), the following statement, or statements, will be executed. If the expression evaluates to false, the wait statement will delay execution of the following statement, or statements, until the expression does evaluate to true.

Examples:

```
wait (Go==1);
wait (Ld==1) Q <= D;
```

6.4 OPERATORS

ARITHMETIC

Verilog supports the following built-in arithmetic operators. The modulus, "%", operator returns the remainder of the first operand divided by the second operand, where the result has the same sign as the first operand. The power, "**", operator will return the value of the first operand raised to the value of the second operand. For example, "*a* ** *b*" means *a* raised to the power of *b*, or a^b. Note that the division, modulus, and power operators are not synthesizable by many synthesis tools.

- + : addition
- - : subtraction
- * : multiplication
- / : division
- % : modulus
- ** : power

Examples:

```
S <= A + B;
I_reg <= I_reg - 1;
Mulout <= A * B;
```

BITWISE

Verilog supports the following built-in bitwise operators. A ***bitwise operator*** will perform the specified operation bit by bit for the input operands.

- **&** : bitwise AND
- | : bitwise OR
- ^ : bitwise XOR
- ^~ or ~^ : bitwise XNOR
- ~ : bitwise NOT

Examples:

```
F <= X & Y; // Each bit of F is the AND of the
            // corresponding bits of X and of Y
W <= K & P & ~S;
F <= ~X;
```

CONCATENATION

The ***concatenation operator***, "*{ }*", joins bits from two or more expressions, which are separated by commas within the curly brackets. A concatenation may also include a ***replication operator*** used to replicate a value within a concatenation. The replication operator is specified as a positive constant expression preceding one or more expressions enclosed within curly brackets. Concatenation may also be applied to the left side of an assignment statement to concatenate one or more variables within curly braces to which the result of the right-side expression will be assigned.

Examples:

```
A5 = {1'b0, A};
B5 = {1'b0, B};
B5 = {B[3], B};
{Co, S} <= A + B + Ci;

// The following are equivalent
```

```
S <= {A, A, A};
S <= {3{A}};
```

CONDITIONAL

The ***conditional operator*** "*?*", also known as a ***ternary operator*** because it involves three operands, is used as follows: "*A ? B : C*". If *A* is true (non-zero), the operator result is *B*. If *A* is false (zero), the operator result is *C*. An expression is said to evaluate to ***true*** if that expression evaluates to any non-zero value. The conditional operator is commonly used to replace a simple *if-else* statement pattern, and is especially useful because it can appear within expressions where *if-else* statements cannot.

Examples:

```
assign Q = Oe ? R :  32'hZZZZZZZZ;
ABS = (IntVal>=0)?IntVal:-IntVal;
```

EQUALITY

Verilog supports the following built-in equality operators. The four equality operators compare the input operands bit by bit returning true (*1*), if comparison succeeds or returning false (*0*), if the comparison fails. The logical equality, "==", and logical inequality, "*!*=", operators will return an unknown value, *x*, if any of the bits within the input operand are unknown (*x*) or high-impedance (*z*). To handle comparison involving unknown or high-impedance values, the logical equality, "===", and logical inequality, "*!*==", operators should be used.

- == : logical equality
- *!*= : logical inequality
- === : logical equality, including *x* and *z* bits
- *!*== : logical inequality, including *x* and *z* bits

Examples:

```
if (Rst == 1)
   Q <= 4'b0000;

if (Q_s !== 32'h000000FF)
   $display("Failed output enabled");
```

LOGICAL

Verilog supports the following built-in logical operators. In contrast to bitwise operators that operate on corresponding bits of operands and may yield multi-bit results, logical operators treat each operand as a single value that is either true (non-zero) or false (*0*), and return a single value that is either true (*1*), false (*0*), or unknown (*x*) depending on the result of the logical comparison. If any of the bits within the input operands are unknown (*x*) or high-impedance (*z*), the logical operator will return the unknown value, *x*.

- ***!*** : logical negation
- ***&&*** : logical AND
- || : logical OR

Examples:

```
if (Sum>=4 && I==0) begin
   Sum <= 0;
end

for (I=0; !(I>255); I=I+1) begin
   Sum = Sum + ABS(A[I] - B[I]);
end
```

REDUCTION

Verilog supports the following unary reduction operators that perform the specified bitwise operation on the individual bits of the single input operand and returns a 1-bit result. Note that the reduction operators use the same symbols as the corresponding bitwise operators, but are specified as a single operand following the operator.

- ***&*** : reduction AND
- | : reduction OR
- ^ : reduction XOR
- ~***&*** : reduction NAND
- ~| : reduction NOR
- ^~ or ~^ : reduction XNOR

Examples:

```
F <= &X;
W <= ~|Reg32;
Parity <= ^Data_In;
```

RELATIONAL

Verilog supports the following built-in relational operators. The four relational operators will return true (*1*) if the comparison is true and will return false (*0*) if the comparison is false. If any of the bits within the input operands are unknown, *x*, or high-impedance, *z*, the relational operator will return the unknown value, *x*.

- > : greater than
- < : less than
- >= : greater than or equal
- <= : less than or equal

Examples:

```
// For loop with relational operator
// within loop condition expression
for (I=0; I<=255; I=I+1) begin
   Sum = Sum + ABS(A[I] - B[I]);
end

// if-else-if statement using relational
// operators in the if and else-if conditions
if ($signed({1'b0,A}) < B) begin
   Gt <= 0; Eq <= 0; Lt <= 1;
end
else if ($signed({1'b0,A}) > B) begin
   Gt <= 1; Eq <= 0; Lt <= 0;
end
else begin
   Gt <= 0; Eq <= 1; Lt <= 0;
end
```

SHIFT

Verilog supports the following built-in shift operators. The logical right and left shift operators, “>>” and “<<”, shift the first operand by the number of bit locations specified by the second operand, filling in the most significant or least significant bit positions with *0*. The arithmetic left shift operator, “<<<”, shifts the first operand left by the number of bit locations specified by the second operand, filling in the least significant bit positions with *0*. The arithmetic right shift operator, “>>>”, shifts the first operand right by the number of bit locations specified by the second operand, filling in the most significant bit positions with the original value of the most significant bit, in order to retain the sign.

- >> : logical right shift
- << : logical left shift
- >>> : arithmetic right shift
- <<< : arithmetic left shift

Examples:

```
R <= R_in >> 2;
Reg <= Reg <<< 8;
```

OPERATOR PRECEDENCE

Operator precedence in Verilog is defined by several precedence levels. All operators within the same precedence level have the same precedence and are evaluated from left to right. The following lists the Verilog precedence levels from highest to lowest precedence and the operators defined within each precedence level.

- Unary Operators: +, -, !, ~, &, ~&, |, ~|, ^, ~^, ^~
- Power: **
- Multiplication/Division: *, /, %
- Addition/Subtraction: +, -
- Shift: <<, >>, <<<, >>>
- Relational: <, <=, >, >=
- Equality: ==, !=, ===, !==
- Bitwise AND: &
- Bitwise XOR/XNOR: ^, ^~, ~^
- Bitwise OR: |
- Logical AND: &&
- Logical OR: ||
- Conditional: ?
- Concatenation/Replication: {}, { {} }

6.5 SYSTEM TASKS AND FUNCTIONS

Tasks and functions are procedures that are called from within a description. A ***function*** is a procedure having at least one argument, returning a value, and not having any time-controlling statements like delay control or event control. A ***task*** is a procedure having any number of arguments (including none), no return value, and possibly containing time-controlling statements. A function may be thought of as a (possibly complex) computation of a value, whereas a task is an activity itself. A function may itself call other functions, but may not call a task (because that task might have time-controlling statements). A task may call either functions or tasks.

System tasks and ***system functions*** are built-in procedures that interacts with the simulator and/or the simulator's host computer system, to carry out behaviors like writing to a display, reading from a file, or obtaining the current simulation time. System tasks and functions begin with a *$* to distinguish them from regular tasks and functions. The following section will introduce several commonly used system tasks and functions.

$DISPLAY AND $WRITE

The ***$display*** system task is commonly called with a string argument, such as *$display("Hello")*, which would print the word *Hello*, automatically followed by a newline. The ***$write*** system task operates the same as the *$display* task except a newline will not automatically be printed. The *$display* task's string argument is printed literally, except when the special character sequence, "%" followed by a single format specification character, appears in the string. Each occurrence of this special character sequence must be accompanied by a corresponding argument within the *$display* task after the string argument separated by commas. The *$display* system task will print the corresponding argument in place of the special character sequence. The ***format specification*** specifies how the corresponding argument will be printed. The following format specifications are allowed:

- *%c* or *%C* : display ASCII character
- *%d* or *%D* : display decimal value
- *%h* or *%H* : display hexadecimal value
- *%o* or *%O* : display octal value
- *%b* or %B : display binary value
- *%t* or *%T* : display time value
- *%s* or *%S* : display string
- *%l* or *%L* : display library binding
- *%v* or *%V* : display net signal strength
- *%m* or *%M* : display hierarchical module name *(no argument)*
- *%u* or *%U* : display without formatting as binary data (*0* or *1*)
- *%z* or *%Z* : display without formatting as binary data (*0*, *1*, *X*, *Z*)

Several additional special sequences are defined for printing special characters, including:

- *\t* : tab character

- *\n* : newline character
- \\ : backslash character, \
- \" : quotation character, "
- *%%* : percent sign character, %

Examples:

```
$display("Hello");
$display("Failed case %d.", Index);
$display("%t: Reset failed", $time);
$write("No newline will be printed.");
```

FILE INPUT AND OUTPUT

$fopen

The ***$fopen*** system function opens a file for access. Its first argument is the file name of the file on the host system to be opened. Its second argument is the file access type, which can be "*r*" for read, "*w*" for write, or "*a*" for append, in this case being "*r*". The function returns an integer that identifies the opened file to later file-access procedures. Such identification is necessary because there may be more than one file opened at a given time. If the file could not be opened (perhaps due to being non-existent or due to incorrect permissions), the function returns *0*.

Examples:

```
FileId = $fopen("vectors.txt", "r");
if (FileId == 0)
   $display("Could not open input file.");
```

$feof

The ***$feof*** system function returns *0* if the end of the file, whose identifier is specified as an argument, has not yet been reached.

Examples:

```
while ($feof(FileId) == 0) begin
   // Loop statements
end
```

$fgetc

The ***$fgetc*** system function returns the next character in the specified file and returns a 9-bit value. If an error occurred or the end of the file has been reached, the returned value will be *111111111* (which is -1 in decimal). Otherwise, the function will return the read character as a 9-bit value, with the read character in the lower 8 bits and *0* in the high-order bit.

$fclose

The ***$fclose*** system task closes the specified previously-opened file.

Example:

```
$fclose(FileId);
```

$fdisplay and $fwrite

The ***$fdisplay*** and ***$fwrite*** system functions operate the same as the *$display* and *$write* systems functions, respectively, writing the resulting output to the specified file, whose identifier is specified as the first argument.

Examples:

```
$fdisplay(FileId, "Hello");
$fdisplay(FileId, "Failed case %d.", Index);
$fdisplay(FileId, "%t: Reset failed", $time);
$fwrite(FileId, "No newline will be printed.");
```

$readmemb and $readmemh

$readmemh, and ***$readmemb***, are system tasks intended to initialize memories, by reading a file of hex, or binary, numbers (with the file name being the function's first argument) and placing each number into successive elements of an array (with the array name being the second argument). The number of numbers in the file should match the number of elements in the array. The hex numbers in the file should not have a size or base format, and should be separated by white spaces. An address specification may also appear within the file indicating that subsequent values read from the file should be loaded into memory starting at the specified address. The address specification is defined as "@" immediately followed by the target address specified as a hexadecimal number.

Examples:

```
$readmemh("MemA.txt", SADMemA.Memory);
$readmemb("MemBinary.txt", Memory);
```

$SIGNED AND $UNSIGNED

The ***$signed*** and ***$unsigned*** system functions change the interpretation of a specified value from unsigned to signed, and from unsigned to signed, respectively.

Examples:

```
if ($signed({1'b0,A}) < B) begin
   Gt <= 0; Eq <= 0; Lt <= 1;
end
```

$TIME

The ***$time*** system function returns the present simulation time.

Example:

```
$display("%t: Reset failed", $time);
```

6.6 COMMON DATA TYPES

ARRAY

An ***array*** is a multi-dimensional object that groups together multiple elements of the same data type. An array of variables or nets can be declared by specifying the ***array element address range*** after the net or reg variable declaration. The array element address range defines the starting and ending addresses for the elements within each dimension of the array. An array element can be accessed using an index specified within brackets following the array net of variable.

Examples:

```
// Array of 4 32-bit elements
reg [31:0] RegFile [0:3];

// Array of 256 8-bit elements
reg [7:0] Memory [0:255];

// Array of 32 1-bit elements
reg A [0:31];

// Two dimensional array of 8x8 32-bit elements
reg [31:0] Mem2D [0:7][0:7];
```

```
Mem2D[0][1]         // Result is 32-bit vector
Mem2D[0][1][2]      // Result is one bit
Mem2D[0][1][15:0]   // Result is 16-bit vector
```

INTEGER

```
integer Name1, Name2, Name3;
```

An ***integer*** variable data type represents a positive or negative value up to 32 bits wide. Strictly speaking, the integer type is not needed in the language, because the reg type could be used instead. The integer type exists to make code more self-documenting, meaning more self-explanatory. The integer type is generally used to represent decimal number quantities that will not become a hardware register. The index variable of a *for* loop is one such quantity, because we expect synthesis to unroll the loop and hence eliminate the index variable from the design.

Examples:

```
integer Sum;
integer I;
```

SIGNED

In Verilog, input and output ports, and reg variables, are interpreted as unsigned values, unless specified as otherwise. The keyword ***signed*** may be added after the keyword *input*, *output*, or *reg*, to cause the values of those data items to be interpreted as signed values within expressions. However, care should be taken to ensure the signed indication is preserved, as many operations will discard the sign indication. For example, a part selection for accessing a subset of bits within a vector always returns an unsigned value.

Examples:

```
input signed [3:0] B;
reg signed [3:0] B_s;
```

VECTOR

A ***vector*** data type defines a collection of bits, and is more convenient than declaring each bit separately. The vector declaration must specify the numbering and order of the bits using a ***range specification***. A range specification defines the vector's most significant bit position, least significant bit position, ordering of the bits within the vector, as well as implicitly defining the number of bits within the vector. For example, the output vector declaration "*output [3:0] Q;*" defines a vector *Q* with the range specification *[3:0]*. In this example, *[3:0]* means the bits are numbered 3, 2, 1, 0, and thus there are four bits. We could have numbered the bits *[0:3],* or even *[1:4]*, but convention usually puts the highest-order bit on the left and numbering typically begins at 0.

To access an individual bit of a vector, we use a a ***bit selection*** by specifying the bit position in brackets, e.g., *Q[2]* <= *I[1]* would assign input bit 1 to output bit 2. Multiple bits within a vector can be accessed using a ***part selection*** by specifying the highest and lowest bits potion within parentheses separated by a colon. The result of a part selection is always an unsigned vector.

Examples:

```
output [3:0] S;
input [7:0] A, B;
output [31:0] SAD_Out;
reg [31:0] R;

// The following expressions result in the same
// 4-bit vector
A[4:1]
{A[4], A[3], A[2], A[1]}
```

Index

A

R

T

U

V

W